WHOLE
AGAIN

A fresh collection of wholesome recipes

Beatnik

WHOLE
AGAIN

A fresh collection of wholesome recipes

Created by **Bronwyn Kan**

To my beautiful friend, Jase Corliss, thank you for
the years you graced my life with your heart of
gold and words of wisdom. You are ever present
with me and very much a part of this book too.

First published in 2019 by Beatnik Publishing
Text: © Beatnik Publishing 2019
Design and Typesetting: © Beatnik Publishing 2019
Creative direction & Design: Bronwyn Kan
Cover: © Beatnik Publishing 2019
Photography: © Bronwyn Kan 2019

Printed and bound in China using Forestry Stewardship Council ™
(FSC ™) - certified paper and other controlled material

ISBN 978-0-9951180-2-7

PO Box 8276, Symonds Street,
Auckland 1150, New Zealand
www.beatnikpublishing.com

Introduction

At its very heart, my previous book **WHOLE: Recipes for Simple Wholefood Eating** celebrated a community of women who ignited a conversation on the topic of food, health and wellness. It has been truly amazing to witness how much it has influenced not only me but those all around me. In the years that have since passed, I've also continued to find myself drawn to seeking out and nurturing new friendships and connections with those who are just as passionate about inspiring change.

So here I am, beyond excited to share with you another epic collaboration and collection of recipes. These wholesome, delectable recipes have been shared by our ever-growing community of entrepreneurs who are devoted to educating and encouraging us to eat well while caring for the world that we live in. They have come into my life (as well as yours I'm sure!) through time spent wandering around at weekend markets, attending talks and events, scouting for new food experiences, and, of course, connecting through mutual friends and on social media. I am endlessly in admiration of these individuals and I have had, no doubt, an awe-inspiring adventure filled with travel and plenty of good food enjoyed in good company.

Those who know me know that I would happily devote many hours in a kitchen to create the ultimate treat or a family feast. More often than not, however, life calls for food that is good yet simple, and I appreciate it just as much. You will find a bit of both gathered in this book but all the recipes remain centred on wholefoods and are in no way strict in their approach – which is how I choose to fuel my body. I encourage you and hope that you feel empowered to substitute as you wish or need and work with the ingredients you have on hand – it is a truly satisfying way to cook.

So dive in. Take your pick of which superfood sweet treat to whip up next or perhaps you're after a warm, hearty bowl to add to the dinner table. This book is for you - embrace it, let it guide you and inspire you to get a little creative with ingredients that have now found their place in the modern pantry.

With love,
Bronwyn

Contents

Monique Hemmingson

WILD ONE WHOLEFOODS

Mount Maunganui, Bay of Plenty
@_wlder_

With Green Goddess smoothies in hand and Remy the retrodoodle pup by our side, Monique Hemmingson and I find a quiet spot out back in the sun drenched courtyard of her now former wholefoods eatery to settle into.

Upon her return to New Zealand from London in 2016, Monique threw open the doors to her own wholefoods café, Wild One, here in the heart of Mount Maunganui. With plenty of previous hospitality experience under her belt and fresh, nourishing food on offer, the café quickly won over the local community as well as the influx of visitors to this vibrant, beachside town in the warmer, summer months. The menu honoured and changed with each season but always boasted plenty of plant-based options to quench your thirst and fill your bellies.

It's a familiar story that Monique shares with me, in that it was her personal wellness journey that sparked this business venture and it all began while backpacking through Southeast Asia a few years prior. Struck by an illness that continued to trouble her for some time and with no real remedy in sight, she decided to pare back her diet and focus on consuming wholefoods in a bid to help heal her body. On the mend but still adhering to a strict diet, Monique, in turn, wanted to encourage and offer others the opportunity to consciously enjoy food that benefited both themselves and their environment - no matter what diet they embraced.

Three years on and Monique has swapped the fast-paced café scene for a new adventure. Her love for the outdoors and wellness were once embodied in the plant-based fare and down-to-earth decor that adorned the space of Wild One. Now, she spends her time travelling and writing with those same passions as her compass.

SWEET CHILLI TEMPEH RICE PAPER ROLLS

This fresh take on Vietnamese rolls is definitely one to note down for a light and easy dinner. The crunch of peanuts, hint of heat in the sweet chilli, and creamy satay dip will make your taste buds sing.

MAKES 8-10 ROLLS

250g tempeh, *sliced thinly*

1 Tbsp olive oil

2 Tbsp sweet chilli sauce

50g vermicelli noodles

One packet of rice paper

Handful of fresh mint leaves

⅛ red cabbage, *sliced*

1 carrot, *julienned*

½ capsicum, *sliced*

¼ cucumber, *sliced*

½ avocado, *sliced*

3 Tbsp peanuts, *toasted*

Satay Sauce

1 Tbsp peanut butter

2 Tbsp sweet chilli sauce

3 Tbsp coconut oil, *melted*

1 tsp soy sauce

2 Tbsp coconut cream

Pinch of salt

On medium to high heat, fry your sliced tempeh in olive oil until golden and brown. Add the sweet chilli sauce coating the tempeh pieces well. Fry for a minute or two until you get a sticky consistency then set aside.

Cook the vermicelli by placing the noodles into boiling water and covering for 3-5 minutes until they soften.

Submerge one sheet of rice paper at a time into luke warm water. Leave until the paper becomes clear and soft. Drain the water off and place on a dry board or surface.

In the centre of the rice paper, lay a few small leaves of mint followed by a few slices of cabbage, carrot, capsicum, cucumber, avocado, and 1-2 slices of tempeh. Top with a few strands of rice noodles and a pinch of peanuts. Fold the ends of your rice paper sheet in first then roll the paper up as tightly as you can. Repeat until you have used up all your toppings.

To make the satay dipping sauce, mix all the sauce ingredients together, adding a small amount of boiling hot water to thin out as required.

Serve the rice paper rolls alongside the satay dipping sauce.

MAPLE ROASTED PUMPKIN + TAHINI BOWL

A big abundant salad bowl is my favourite go-to over summer. The crunch of the cabbage and roasted chickpeas, the sweetness of cherry tomatoes, and creaminess of the avocado and tahini equals perfection.

SERVES 1

5-6 pieces of pumpkin, *sliced*

Olive oil, *for drizzling and cooking*

2 Tbsp maple syrup

½ cup (100g) chickpeas, *drained and rinsed*

2 Tbsp pumpkin seeds

2 Tbsp sunflower seeds

2 handfuls of baby spinach

2 handfuls of kale, *stalks removed*

2 cloves of garlic, *finely diced*

2 Tbsp sesame seeds

½ an avocado, *peeled*

Handful of cherry tomatoes, *halved*

¼ red onion, *thinly sliced*

⅛ red cabbage, *thinly sliced*

½ yellow capsicum, *chopped*

Handful of sprouts

Tahini, *to drizzle*

Salt and pepper, *to taste*

Preheat oven to 180°C and line two baking trays with baking paper.

Place pumpkin slices flat in a single layer on one tray. Drizzle with oil and maple syrup.

Lay the chickpeas flat on the other tray. Place both the pumpkin slices and chickpeas in the oven and bake for about 35 -40 minutes.

While your pumpkin and chickpeas are in the oven, place pumpkin seeds and sunflower seeds in a dry pan on high heat. Wait until the pumpkin seeds start to pop and crackle. Watch closely as they will burn easily. Once done, remove from heat and stir in ½ tsp of olive oil, salt and pepper.

Sauté your spinach and kale in a saucepan on high heat with garlic, olive oil, salt and pepper - this will only take a few minutes so stir regularly and keep a close eye. Once they begin to wilt, remove from heat.

Place the sesame seeds in a bowl and gently roll the avocado in it till it is covered in seeds.

In a big bowl, arrange your pumpkin, chickpeas, spinach, kale, avocado, cherry tomatoes, onion, cabbage, capsicum and a handful of sprouts. Drizzle tahini generously across the top and serve.

CHOCOLATE FUDGE PANCAKES

These decadent pancakes have a deliciously fudgey texture
and when served with the slight bitterness of berries and
smooth creamy yoghurt, create a guilt-free breakfast trifecta.

MAKES 10 MEDIUM PANCAKES

1 cup (103g) ground almonds

1 cup (156g) buckwheat flour

½ cup (94g) coconut sugar

¼ tsp baking soda

¼ tsp baking powder

¼ cup (24g) cacao powder

1 cup (250ml) almond milk

2 Tbsp coconut oil, *for cooking*

Linseed 'Eggs'

2 Tbsp ground linseed

¼ cup (60ml) warm water

Combine the ground almonds, buckwheat flour, coconut sugar,
baking soda, baking powder and cacao powder into a food
processor and blitz briefly until mixed well.

In a separate bowl, make your linseed eggs by combining the
ground linseed and roughly ¼ cup of warm water until you get
an egg-like consistency.

Add your linseed eggs and almond milk to the dry mix and blend
in a food processor until smooth.

Heat up a pan and grease with a little bit of coconut oil. Pour
the mixture and cook for 2-3 minutes each side until lightly
browned.

Serve with your favourite coconut yoghurt dolloped on top with
a mix of fresh seasonal berries.

TIP – *If you have the time, leave the pancake mix in the fridge
for a few hours prior to cooking it. This helps the mix set and will
create fluffier, thicker pancakes.*

Mike + Chantel Priddy

GREENLEAF ORGANICS

Kingsland, Auckland
greenleaforganics.co.nz | @greenleaforganics

It's no easy feat juggling running a business and raising two little ones but husband and wife duo Mike and Chantel Priddy show no signs of slowing down. Together, they grew their brand Greenleaf Organics into one of Auckland's favourite wholefood, organic cafés. Now, they've set their sights on encouraging more Kiwis to switch to drinking Switchel.

Their wellness journey started with their son Rocco who became troubled with food allergies as a baby. They discovered that consuming more organic produce played a key role in helping to alleviate his symptoms and began to instil the importance of eating well in their young family. This also led to Mike and Chantel making the move back to Auckland from Sydney to help Mike's sister, Sarah, run Greenleaf Organics in a desire to help educate and provide nourishment to the wider community.

Greenleaf Organics quickly blossomed from delivering smoothies into a sleek café that found its home tucked away inside an industrial space on New North Road, Kingsland. Enter through a garage roller door and splashes of colour, geometric shapes and artwork decorated the polished concrete walls. It was a café loved by many for the organic, innovative, hearty range of food and drink on offer to help fuel their busy days.

Mike and Chantel have moved on from the day-to-day running of the café to pour their heart and soul into developing their award-winning line of tonics - Switchel, GLO shots and GLO brew. Handmade and bottled on-site, their signature drinks are apple cider vinegar based and uniquely blended with organic juices such as turmeric, beetroot and pineapple. It's a hard choice but today I settle on an immune-boosting bottle of Grapefruit Switchel and Rocco happily cracks right into one too.

Mike and Chantel's focus was and still is simple - to provide an organic, functional product for everyone to enjoy, and these sweet nectars will no doubt have you glowing inside and out.

ROASTED BERBERE VEGETABLE SALAD

This could possibly be the easiest, tastiest and most versatile salad you can make. With baked seasonal vegetables tossed through Ethiopian berbere spice, this can be served both warm or cold.

SERVES 4, AS A SIDE

2 beetroot, *diced*

2 zucchini, *roughly chopped*

½ pumpkin, *diced*

1 kūmara, *roughly chopped*

1 onion, *roughly chopped*

2 tsp salt

3 garlic cloves, *diced*

¼ cup (60ml) olive oil

3 Tbsp berbere spice

Coconut Yoghurt Labneh

1 cup (250ml) coconut yoghurt

Juice of 1 lemon

2 tsp salt

Drizzle of olive oil

To serve

Rocket leaves

Micro greens

Equipment

Cheese cloth

To make the coconut yoghurt labneh, combine the first three ingredients and place in cheese cloth overnight until firm. Top with olive oil and store in the fridge and serve as needed.

Preheat oven to 180°C and line a baking tray with baking paper.

Toss all the cut vegetables together in a large bowl with oil and spices.

Spread the vegetables out on the tray and bake in the oven for 30 minutes. Turn and cook for a further 30 minutes or until all vegetables are roasted evenly.

Remove from the oven and allow the vegetables to cool.

In a large serving bowl, lay a bed of rocket leaves. Gently toss with the roasted vegetables. Top with small chunks of the coconut yoghurt labneh and micro greens and serve.

BEETROOT + APPLE BIRCHER

Beetroot for breakfast. What!? Makes sense when you combine it with fresh apple and nutritious chia to make a creamy and sumptuous morning-time bircher muesli.

SERVES 1

1 cup (90g) rolled oats

1 cup (250ml) coconut milk

½ cup (125ml) beetroot and apple juice

1 Tbsp chia seeds

1 tsp cinnamon

¼ tsp nutmeg

1 Tbsp maple syrup

1 tsp Greenleaf Organics GLObrew beetroot and ginger latte powder or ground ginger

To serve

1 Tbsp coconut yoghurt

½ an apple, *shredded*

Handful of mint leaves

Handful of micro greens

Maple syrup, *to drizzle*

Combine all the bircher ingredients in a bowl and cover. Refrigerate overnight.

To serve the bircher, add coconut yoghurt, apple, mint leaves and micro greens on top and drizzle maple syrup.

VIETNAMESE BANH GOI (SAMOSA)

These require some attention but will repay you with crispy and flavoursome morsels. Enjoy these samosas for lunch or dinner, on their own or with a salad. Yes please!

MAKES 12 SAMOSAS

200g purple kūmara, *boiled*

200g mushrooms *(a mix of button, oyster or cauliflower), sliced*

1 cup (100g) Chinese cabbage, *grated*

1 tsp salt

1 tsp pepper

1 onion, *chopped*

¼ cup leek, *chopped*

½ cup walnuts, *roughly chopped*

1 tsp garlic, *crushed*

1 tsp ginger, *grated*

½ tsp garlic powder

½ tsp onion powder

½ tsp cordyceps (mushroom powder)

2 tsp Chinese five spice

½ cup (118ml) sesame oil

6 sheets puff pastry

Olive oil, *for brushing and cooking*

Milk, *for brushing*

¼ cup (40g) sesame seeds

Dipping Sauce

1 cup (110g) blackberries

½ cup (118ml) grapeseed oil

1 Tbsp hemp seed oil

1 Tbsp maple syrup

2 Tbsp white wine vinegar

1 Tbsp tamari

Roughly mash boiled kūmara with a fork and set aside.

Preheat oven to 180°C and line a baking tray with baking paper.

Heat a pan over medium heat and fry mushrooms in some olive oil then set aside.

In same pan, fry cabbage and sprinkle with salt and pepper. Then place in the same bowl as the mushrooms.

Fry onion and leek along with walnuts, all the spices and sesame oil. Add this to the mushroom, kūmara and cabbage and set aside to slightly cool.

Cut each sheet of puff pastry into four triangles and place a spoonful of filling into the middle. Brush the edges of the sheet with your choice of milk. Fold over to create a triangle and press the sides down with a fork. Brush the top with a little olive oil and sprinkle sesame seeds on top.

Bake for 20 minutes in the oven or until golden brown.

To make the dipping sauce, blend all ingredients together in a high speed blender.

Serve immediately while hot alongside the dipping sauce.

Emily Hope

HOPE NUTRITION

Blenheim, Marlborough
hopenutrition.org.nz | @hopenutrition

Marlborough – a region close to my heart and one I always love to come back to. I made my way here to the South Island of New Zealand a few years back and stopped by to visit Emily Hope. We bonded over a day spent in her kitchen baking a luscious lemon loaf. On that day, Emily also threw together for lunch a warming, nourishing Buddha bowl from what we could find in her pantry and harvest from out amongst her family's vegetable garden in the middle of winter. I knew then that this was a woman who loved to embrace good, simple food.

Hailing from the beautiful rural town of Blenheim, Emily discovered a love for good food and health when she first pursued studies in nutrition at Otago University. After seizing the opportunity to spend time abroad in Northern Italy with her husband Jonny, they later returned to Auckland where Emily continued to work within the public health nutrition sector before relocating back to her hometown. It is here that she now runs her own nutrition practice, Hope Nutrition, out of a cosy log cabin-turned-office that sits only a few strides away from her family home. For a few months of the year, you'll also find her lending a helping hand on her parents' bountiful fig and feijoa orchard, Old Road Estate – all while raising her two young children, Isabella and Louie.

From the olive oil she uses daily in her cooking to the goat's cheese delightfully crumbled on top of her fig, hazelnut and pomegranate salad, Emily could tell you exactly where it came from and who made it – I adore her passion for choosing to support the local producers (like herself) that surround her. I've been lucky enough this time round to catch a sight of her family's homegrown fresh figs, in all their glory, hanging off the trees in the orchard out back. Even little Isabella knows and proudly declares to her mum that *"Poppa's figs are the best!"*

MATCHA CREAMED BROWN RICE PORRIDGE

This gluten-free version made with leftover cooked brown rice is a delicious and wholesome way to start your day. Topped with granola for some hearty crunch and seasonal fruit, it will keep you going all morning.

SERVES 1

⅓ cup brown rice, *cooked and cooled*

⅓ cup water, *recently boiled*

⅓ cup coconut cream or milk of your choice

1 Tbsp maple syrup or honey

1 Tbsp desiccated coconut

1 Tbsp smooth peanut butter

½ tsp matcha powder

To serve

Fresh or frozen berries

Granola

Dollop of coconut cream

Black sesame seeds

Combine the brown rice, water, coconut cream, maple syrup, coconut, peanut butter and matcha powder in a small pot.

Bring to the boil, stirring, and then lower the heat and simmer for 10-15 minutes or until thickened to your liking. Stir the porridge frequently to ensure it doesn't stick or burn.

Pour the porridge into a serving bowl and top with berries, granola, coconut cream and black sesame seeds.

COCONUT CREAM PIE SLICE

Perfect for those who LOVE coconut! This is a lovely wee recipe to add to your baking repertoire that's not only ridiculously simple but also completely delicious.

MAKES ABOUT 16 SLICES

Base

¼ cup (43g) dried pitted dates, *soaked in boiling water for 10 minutes*

½ cup (87g) Medjool dates, *pitted*

¼ cup (25g) cacao powder

1 cup (140g) raw almonds

2 Tbsp coconut oil, *melted*

Topping

2 cans good-quality thick coconut cream *(place in the fridge to set then remove 10 minutes prior to use)*

½ tsp cinnamon

¼ tsp vanilla extract

2 Tbsp maple syrup

Handful of cacao nibs, *to garnish*

Handful of freeze-dried whole plums or raspberries, *to garnish*

Squeeze out the water from the dried dates and place into a food processor or blender along with the Medjool dates, cacao powder, almonds and coconut oil. Blend on high until all ingredients are combined.

Line a square pan with baking paper and spread the mixture into pan so that you form a base layer. Place into the freezer to set while you make the topping.

To make the topping, scoop out the thick part of the coconut cream from both cans and place it into a medium bowl. Add the cinnamon, vanilla and pure maple syrup and mix until thoroughly combined.

Remove base from the freezer and pour the topping over the base and spread out evenly with the back of a spoon.

Evenly scatter over cacao nibs and whole freeze-dried plums or raspberries, crushing them with your hand as you go.

Return to the fridge to set for at least 30 minutes before slicing into squares and serving.

Keep any leftover slices refrigerated.

FIG, HAZELNUT + POMEGRANATE SALAD

We absolutely adore fig season around here. Not only is our family orchard in full swing but we get the pleasure of feasting on this forbidden fruit morning, noon and night! Rich in fibre, calcium and antioxidants, figs pair beautifully with toasted hazelnuts and velvety goat's cheese.

SERVES 6, AS A SIDE

6 cups (450g) mixed salad
   leaves *(such as rocket, mesclun or
   watercress)*

6 fresh figs, *sliced*

100g goat's cheese or feta,
   crumbled

½ cup (75g) salted hazelnuts,
   toasted

½ a pomegranate, *seeds only*

Dressing

3 Tbsp olive oil

Juice of 1 lemon

Salt and pepper, *to taste*

To serve

Drizzle of honey, *optional*

To make the dressing, combine the olive oil, lemon juice, salt and pepper in a small jar with a lid. Shake until well combined.

In a large mixing bowl, toss the salad leaves with the dressing by hand. Ensure the greens are evenly coated.

Place the greens onto a serving plate and scatter over sliced figs, goat's cheese, hazelnuts and pomegranate seeds. Drizzle over honey if using just before serving.

TIP – *If you don't have hazelnuts, toasted and salted walnuts are equally as delicious to use in this salad.*

Cameron Sims

PLANT CULTURE

Auckland
plantculture.nz | @_plantculture

No one wholeheartedly sings praises for hemp like Cameron Sims does. Upon discovering the powerful health benefits of this superfood a couple years back, Cam embarked on a journey that led him to start up his own social enterprise, Plant Culture, supplying premium hemp seed products to the masses in New Zealand.

Hemp is a plant that has been around for thousands of years and is incredibly versatile, yet its properties and nutritional value are still widely met with confusion. Dispelling its stigma is a part of what drives Cam and he also views it as the perfect spark to lead the way to inspiring change in our culture.

Cam - who greets everyone with nothing less than bounds of energy and enthusiasm - was raised on a sheep and beef farm in Wairarapa. Now, he is proudly an advocate of a plant-based lifestyle and loves nothing more than working with hemp. Over the years, he has hosted a TEDx talk on the sustainable future that hemp offers, launched pop-up restaurants that showcase the mighty ingredient on his menu and also worked in collaboration with other chefs, all in a bid to give everyone a taste of the food of the future.

My day with Cam in the kitchen turns into an impromptu taste testing session and it astounds me all the ways he's experimented with the unique super seed ingredient. I try a spoonful of hemp ice cream that he whips out of the freezer and sip on some freshly made hemp milk, and a good slather of hemp butter accompanies my avocado toast for lunch. He's even played with the idea of hemp sausages - it's evident that his obsession with the humble hemp seed runs deep and he's excited about demonstrating just how easy it can be to incorporate it into our diets and lifestyles. His ultimate goal? To make hemp an every day ingredient in the Kiwi household.

HEMP MILK BUTTER

Hemp seed is a staple in the regenerative diet. You can spread this on toast or blend with water to make your own hemp milk. An evolution in a jar with many applications in baking, sauces, smoothies.

MAKES 1 CUP

1 cup (170g) of hemp hearts

4 Tbsp hemp oil or coconut oil

Pinch of salt

Combine hemp hearts with hemp oil and salt in a food processor or high speed blender.

Blend on high for 5 minutes, or until creamy, stopping regularly to scrape down the sides of the blender. You may need to add more oil as you go.

Enjoy fresh or store in the fridge to enjoy over a few months.

CACAO HEMP LOAF

Serve this fresh or toasted, topped with hemp butter, sliced banana and maple syrup for the ultimate experience. Once it's baked and cooled, you can also slice and hide it in the freezer for quick and easy toast!

MAKES 1 LOAF

1 ½ cups (370ml) water

3 Tbsp hemp seed oil or
   coconut oil, *melted*

1 tsp vanilla extract or paste

¾ cup (100g) Plant Culture hemp
   seed protein

1 cup (100g) cacao powder

⅔ cup (100g) sunflower seeds

⅔ cup (90g) flax seeds

½ cup (65g) hazelnuts, almonds
   or hemp seeds

1 cup (100g) buckwheat or rolled
   oats

½ cup (100g) coconut sugar

2 Tbsp chia seeds

4 Tbsp psyllium husk (*3 Tbsp if
   using psyllium husk powder*)

1 tsp salt

Serve with

Hemp Milk Butter, *see page 45*

Banana, *sliced*

In a bowl, whisk together water, hemp seed oil and vanilla extract.

In a big bowl, combine all dry ingredients then mix in liquids.

Before it sets, add mixture to flexible, silicone loaf pan or a standard loaf pan lined with baking paper. (If the dough is too thick to stir, add one or two teaspoons of water until the dough is manageable.)

Smooth out the top with the back of a spoon. Let sit out on the counter for at least 2 hours or overnight. To ensure the dough is ready, it should retain its shape even when you pull the sides of the loaf pan away from it or lift the baking paper.

Preheat oven to 180°C.

Place in the oven and bake for 20 minutes. Remove bread from loaf pan, place it upside down directly on the rack and bake for another 30 to 40 minutes. Bread is done when it sounds hollow when tapped. Let cool completely before slicing.

Serve with Hemp Milk Butter spread on top and slices of banana.

Store bread in a tightly sealed container for up to five days or slice the loaf and freeze.

HEMP SEED FUDGE

Melt-in-your-mouth, healthy fudge that tastes like
Russian fudge but without the sugar crash. All you
need to make this is an ice tray, a pot and a spoon.

MAKES 8-12 PIECES

½ cup hulled tahini or hemp
   butter

5 Tbsp hemp seed

3 Tbsp coconut oil or cacao
   butter

3 Tbsp honey

2 tsp vanilla extract

¼ tsp salt

Equipment

Ice tray or silicone moulds

Garnish

Flowers, freeze dried powder,
   berries, or seeds.

Mix all ingredients in a pot on low heat to gently melt and
combine.

Pour mixture into moulds and place in the freezer for at least
30 minutes or until set.

Remove from the moulds, sprinkle with hemp seed or any
garnish of your choice.

Sharna McElligott

THE NOURISHED EATERY

114 Willow Street, Tauranga
thenourishingbaker.com | @thenourishingbaker

She's a gentle yet bravely optimistic soul who hails from the deep south of New Zealand in Invercargill - Sharna McElligott is the girl at the helm of her own business, The Nourished Eatery. Her journey has been far from easy but it sure is an inspiring tale. One that has moulded her into an advocate for supporting locals, determined to achieve a zero-waste business and with a big heart, care for and give back to her community.

Whilst pursuing studies in nutritional medicine in Sydney several years prior, Sharna fell ill and was consequently diagnosed with Chronic Fatigue Syndrome. In her best interest, she decided to return home and take some time off to allow herself to rest. She found solace in baking and an unexpected popularity for her vegan creations on the social media platform Instagram. Before long, Sharna built herself a hole-in-the-wall space that served as her first kitchen and café. Within months she outgrew that location and went in search again for a bigger, better permanent home.

Establishing The Nourished Eatery has, in a significant way, helped Sharna to heal. It has allowed her to continue working, fulfill her passion, and set her own schedule that ensures her health remains a priority. There is time to still fulfill cake orders too - today, she's delicately decorating a decadent chocolate one in front of me with a handful of colourful edible flowers.

Now located in Tauranga's CBD, the beautifully crafted, plant-based food on offer at Sharna's brunch spot will not only put a smile on your face but you can enjoy it knowing that you are looking after yourself and the environment too. Start planning your next trip to the Bay of Plenty and be sure to make room for one of her legendary doughnuts that are 100% vegan and 100% delicious.

SLOW COOKED JACKFRUIT TOASTIE

Slow cooking jackfruit makes it super versatile; you can use it
in burgers, tacos, or in toasties just like the recipe below.

SERVES 4

2 cans of jackfruit in brine or water

1 red or white onion, *finely diced*

3 cloves garlic, *diced*

1 cup (250ml) tomato or BBQ sauce

1 cup (250ml) vegetable broth

1 tsp ground cumin

Pinch of salt

Pinch of pepper

Curried Aioli Dressing

½ cup (112g) sunflower oil

¼ cup (60ml) soy milk

1 tsp curry powder

Juice of ½ a lemon

2 cloves of garlic

Pinch of salt and pepper

Squirt of mustard

To serve

Sourdough bread

Rocket

Tomato

Sprouts

Cheese

Olive oil, *for toasting*

Combine all the jackfruit filling ingredients in a small pot or
slow cooker and cook for 1-4 hours on low heat or until the
jackfruit easily pulls apart resembling pork. The longer you
cook this for the better the result.

To make the curried aioli dressing, blend all the ingredients
in a high powered blender until thick and creamy (about 30
seconds). Store any leftover dressing in a container in the
fridge for 7-12 days.

To make the toastie, spread curried aioli on two slices of
sourdough bread. On one slice of the sourdough, spoon
over the slow cooked jackfruit filling and add your favourite
vegetable toppings. We've used rocket, sliced tomato,
sprouts and cheese. Place the other slice of sourdough on
top to create a sandwhich.

Heat a pan with a bit of olive oil and toast the sandwich lightly
on each side before serving immediately while warm.

BLUE BEAUTY
PASSION SMOOTHIE

Butterfly pea powder has an earthy green tea taste and contains the
antioxidant proanthocyanidin which promotes collagen production.
We love the blue colour it gives our drinks and if you add a squeeze
of lemon it'll even transform into a beautiful purple colour.

SERVES 1

1 banana
2 tsp butterfly pea powder
Flesh of 1 passionfruit
Flesh of 1 kiwifruit
1 cup (250ml) coconut water
   or milk of your choice

Place all the ingredients into a high powered blender
and blend until smooth and creamy.

Pour into a glass and serve.

CHOCOLATE SPELT COOKIES

These cookies have always been a bestseller in the café – they are super soft and pair great with the dark chocolate. You can swap out the spelt flour for plain flour if you don't have it on hand.

MAKES 10-12 COOKIES

½ cup (105g) vegan butter
   or coconut oil

1 cup (150g) coconut sugar

¼ cup (60ml) almond milk
   or your milk of choice

Pinch of salt

1 tsp vanilla extract

2 cups (240g) spelt flour

1 tsp baking powder

1 tsp baking soda

Half a block of 50% dark
   chocolate, *broken into
   small squares*

Preheat oven to 180°C and line a baking sheet with baking paper.

In the bowl of an electric mixer, cream the butter and sugar. Add the milk, salt and vanilla and beat again until combined.

Slowly add in the flour, baking powder and baking soda and mix until smooth.

Using an ice cream scoop, spoon the cookie batter onto the prepared tray keeping them about 3cm apart. Place three squares of chocolate on top of each of the cookies (there is no need to flatten the cookies).

Bake the cookies for 10-12 minutes or until just golden.

Remove from the oven and let cool for a minute before transferring onto a wire rack to further cool.

Keep cookies stored in an airtight container.

Gretta Carney

HAPĪ CLEAN KAI CO-OP

89 Hastings Street, Napier, Hawke's Bay
hapi.nz | @hapinz

Co-founded by Gretta Carney, in December 2015, Hapī Clean Kai Co-Op was established upon the philosophy that what we eat has the ability to heal and nourish our mind, body and spirit – simple but profound.

Their menu is like no other in the small Art Deco town that is Napier. Take your pick from the fridge that is lined with freshly pressed tonics, house-made nut milks and bright jars of fermented goods such as sauerkraut and kimchi. Meanwhile, the cabinets are jam-packed with a selection of raw slices, cheesecakes, bliss balls, and for those looking for a bigger bite, hearty sandwiches and salads beckon.

Gretta believes that our physical and emotional well-being is strongly intertwined with food and that it is important to eat and share food with integrity - which is why they make a passionate and genuine commitment to source and work alongside local suppliers who adhere to similar traditional, organic practices that they embrace while preparing food here at Hapī .

With the sun beating down outside, the deliciously refreshing fizz of the Raspberry Shrub Soda that Gretta has freshly poured for me is going down a treat. And if there was ever a day for it, today is the day to also indulge in a bowl of Hapī's wholesome take on ice cream - sugar-free, vegan coconut soft serve, decorated with toppings and all.

You can count on Gretta and her team to produce an abundance of creative, plant-based kai (food) to keep the locals in Napier as well as the waves of tourists that roll in year-round well-fed. And as it says so beautifully painted on their wall in the small take-out shop, everyone is welcome at Hapī .

FRESH ALMOND MATCHA MILK

Freshly made nut milks are enzyme rich, living milks and thus the perfect vehicle for transporting superfoods like matcha into our cells. Making your own nut milk can be a quick and easy habit acquired by regular practice.

MAKES 1 LITRE

1 cup (140g) almonds

4 cups (1L) filtered water, *plus extra for soaking*

Pinch of salt

1 ½ Tbsp matcha powder

3 Tbsp maple syrup, *or to taste*

Equipment

Nut milk bag or muslin cloth

Cover almonds generously in filtered water and stand in the fridge overnight. Soaking activates the enzymes and removes enzyme inhibitors that can be hard to digest.

Strain soaked nuts and rinse well.

Place nuts into a high powered blender with 1 litre of filtered water and salt and blend on high for 20 seconds, 3 times.

Strain the milk through a nut milk bag or muslin cloth into a large jug.

Pour the strained milk back into the blender along with the matcha powder and maple syrup and pulse briefly until well combined.

Pour the milk into a 1-litre bottle and refrigerate immediately. This will keep in the fridge for about 5 days.

TIP – *It's important to maintain scrupulous hygiene when making nut milks to ensure that they keep well.*

TURMERIC + CHICKEN NOODLE SOUP

A simple and popular soup that really just requires you to make a good broth. Making broth is a quick and easy habit gained by regular practice. The outcome is a restorative superfood rich in bioavailable minerals and collagen that support digestion and build immunity.

SERVES 4

Bone Broth

1-2 roast chicken carcasses

¼ cup (60ml) cider vinegar

1 tsp nettle

1 tsp horsetail

1 tsp kelp

1 large thumb ginger, *finely sliced*

To serve

1 packet of black bean spaghetti,
  or gluten-free noodle of your choice

2 cups cooked chicken, *shredded*

4 Tbsp kimchi

30ml tamari

30ml sesame oil

1-2 Tbsp turmeric, *finely grated*

Salt and pepper, *to taste*

Coriander, *to garnish*

Place all bone broth ingredients in a small crockpot and cover with filtered water. Cook on high for 8 hours or on low overnight. The liquid will reduce by about a quarter.

Alternatively put all ingredients in a small stock pot with a tight fitting lid and generously cover with filtered water. Cover and gently simmer for 8 hours or until liquid reduces by half.

Strain and refrigerate when cool or use whilst hot to make this soup. The broth will keep for 5 days if kept well refrigerated.

To serve, cook noodles according to packet instructions and divide between 4 bowls.

In each bowl, add ½ cup chicken and a tablespoon of kimchi. Season broth with tamari, sesame oil, turmeric, salt and pepper to taste and pour into bowls to cover the chicken.

Garnish with coriander and serve while hot.

RASPBERRY SHRUB SODA

A Shrub is a traditional cider vinegar soda that is flavoured with fruit or herbs. We produce a range of cider vinegar sodas and this brightly coloured fizz is totally our favourite.

MAKES 1 LITRE OF CONCENTRATE

4 cups (500g) raspberries, *fresh or frozen*

1 ½ cups (375ml) cider vinegar

2 cups (500ml) agave syrup

½ cup (125ml) lemon juice

2 tsp (15g) citric acid

To serve

Soda water

Ice

Place raspberries in a jug or jar and pour over cider vinegar. Cover and steep for 8 hours or overnight.

Add agave, lemon juice and citric acid and stir to combine.

To serve, fill a glass with ice and soda water and pour over 1-2 tablespoons of syrup or to taste.

Keep remaining concentrate in a bottle refrigerated.

TIP – *At Hapī we don't strain our raspberries out of the syrup because we like the way they look and taste in the soda. You can also add 10ml rosewater to the recipe to make Rose & Raspberry Shrub Soda.*

HAPĪ CLEAN KAI CO-OP

Luke + Tim Burrows

WISE BOYS

Auckland
wiseboys.nz | @wiseboysnz

Kiwis no doubt love their meat and dairy but these two sustainably minded brothers are changing up the food scene with the launch of their vegan food truck and the crowds are loving it.

An idea dreamt up and then swiftly built in the summer of 2015 by Luke and Tim Burrows, Wise Boys humbly set out to change our perceptions by serving up a fast food menu entirely plant-based yet still lip-smackingly delicious. Formerly a lawyer and engineer respectively, Luke and Tim now devote all their time to expanding their business and dishing out burgers that are good for you and the environment.

Wise Boys first caught my attention when my friend Serge praised their burgers and loved them so much he often ordered more than one for himself at a time. Originally parked at No.1 Queen Street in Auckland, the brothers have now been travelling far and wide in their charming custom built 'burger shack' to feed the masses – be it at markets, festivals, expos or the ever-so-popular private gig at weddings. Keep a look out because they just might pop up in your neighbourhood next.

But if that was proving difficult, you're in luck as the brothers have now secured their first permanent location in the heart of Grey Lynn. You can get your burger fix here any day of the week as well as their legendary fries that are accompanied by a good helping of their much loved vegan aioli.

As Tim goes about stacking and perfecting his towering Spicy Mex burger, I can't help but wonder how anyone could get their mouth around it – but hey, devouring a good burger is bound to get messy right? Luke, on the other hand, with a big grin on his face, can't wait to just tuck right into his.

SPICY MEX VEGAN BURGER

This is a homestyle version of one of our food truck originals. It's a crowd favourite, super filling and flavour heavy! Eat fast though because it can get messy and you might end up with half the burger in your lap.

SERVES 5

1 red onion, *diced*

¼ cup (30g) flour or gluten-free flour

4 Tbsp (25g) ground linseed

1 Tbsp salt

1 Tbsp ground cumin

1 tsp chilli powder

1 tsp ground black pepper

2 cans kidney beans *(440g after drained)*

1 tomato, *diced*

½ mango, *diced*

Fresh coriander, *finely chopped (optional)*

Juice of ½ lemon

Salt and pepper, to taste

To serve

5 burger buns

Chipotle sauce

Relish

Lettuce

Corn chips

1 avocado, *smashed and mixed with the juice of ½ a lemon*

To make burger patty mixture, in a mixing bowl, combine half of the diced onion, flour, linseed, spices and kidney beans. Using your hands, mix all the ingredients together. Leave to sit for at least 15 minutes to allow for binding.

To make salsa, in another bowl, combine the remaining diced onion, tomato, mango and coriander. Season with salt and pepper to taste and squeeze in the juice of ½ a lemon.

Divide the burger patty mixture and form into 5 patties (weighing about 110 grams each).

In a pan over medium–high heat, fry each patty for 10-15 minutes till they are crispy on the outside. Lightly toast the buns in the same pan after you've cooked the patties.

To assemble the burgers, place a spoon of relish on the base of each bun. Then layer the lettuce, a generous spoonful of salsa, a burger patty, a drizzle of chipotle sauce and a few corn chips. On the top half of the bun spread a spoonful of smashed avocado and place on top of the burger.

TERIYAKI TEMPEH + MISO RICE

Tempeh is our favourite way to add some healthy protein to a meal. It has a unique texture which is light and fresh, but still keeps you full. This recipe is easy to execute and makes use of plenty of fresh, colourful vegetables.

SERVES 4

1 thumb of ginger, *grated*

2 cloves garlic, *crushed*

2 Tbsp pure maple syrup

1 Tbsp sesame oil, *plus a few extra drops*

4 Tbsp soy sauce

Juice of 1 orange

400g tempeh, *cut into strips*

2 cups rice

2 Tbsp miso paste

3 cups water, *for cooking*

1 head broccoli, *chopped*

1 red capsicum, *chopped*

1 orange capsicum, *chopped*

1 red onion, *chopped*

Oil, *for cooking*

Salt and pepper, *to taste*

In a wide, shallow bowl, combine ginger, garlic, maple syrup, sesame oil, soy sauce and the juice of half an orange.

Place the tempeh slices in the bowl and cover with marinade. Leave to sit while you prepare the rice and vegetables.

To make the miso rice, combine rice and water in a rice cooker and add miso paste. Stir to ensure miso paste is well mixed in then set to cook.

In a pan over high heat, fry chopped vegetables, add in a few drops of sesame oil and season with salt and pepper to taste. Cook on high heat until the vegetables are slightly charred on the edges then set aside.

In the same pan, fry marinated tempeh slices with a generous amount of oil. Add any remaining marinade to the frying pan. Cook the tempeh on medium to high heat for around 5 minutes on each side.

To serve, place a scoop of rice in each bowl, top with vegetables and a few slices of tempeh. Give a quick squeeze of the remaining half of the orange over each bowl for freshness.

CARAMELISED BEETROOT DIP

WITH SEED CRACKERS

Kelly, who works closely with us, is a hummus fiend (even creating a hummus-rating Instagram page). She loves experimenting with new flavours, so this is her go-to when it comes to a delicious spin on your classic hummus.

Caramelised Beetroot Dip

1 beetroot, *chopped into eighths*

¾ cup (190ml) olive oil

1 Tbsp apple cider vinegar

½ cup (100g) coconut sugar

3 Tbsp tahini

Juice of ½ a lemon

1 can (400g) chickpeas, *drained, rinsed and boiled for about 5 minutes or until softened slightly*

1 clove of garlic

Salt and pepper, *to taste*

Sunflower seeds, *to garnish*

Seed Crackers

⅓ cup (55g) ground linseed

1 ½ cups (375ml) water

1 cup (200g) quinoa, *cooked and cooled*

½ cup (60g) pumpkin seeds

½ cup (70g) sesame seeds

½ cup (67g) sunflower seeds

⅓ cup (54g) chia seeds

Salt, *to taste*

1 tsp ground cumin

1 tsp rosemary

Place beetroot in a pot and boil for 10 minutes or until soft enough to poke into, then drain.

In a pan combine ¼ cup of the olive oil, apple cider vinegar, coconut sugar and salt and pepper. Turn it up to a high heat until it starts to bubble, then add in beetroot and turn down to a low simmering heat. Turn the beetroot over regularly to marinate, do this for about 10-15 minutes.

In a food processor, combine tahini, lemon juice, and remaining ½ cup of olive oil. Blend until emulsified (30 seconds on high). It should reach a fluffy and light consistency.

Add in boiled chickpeas, garlic, beetroot and any remaining sauce in pan, and generous pinches of salt and pepper. Blend again for 45 seconds or until desired consistency, scraping down sides with spatula regularly.

Pour into a serving bowl and garnish with sunflower seeds .

To make the seed crackers, preheat oven to 150°C and line a baking tray with baking paper.

Combine ground linseed and water in a bowl, and let sit covered for about 10 minutes.

Add cooked quinoa and remaining seeds to the wet mix and stir through well. Add in a generous amount of salt, the cumin and rosemary.

Pour the mixture out onto the baking tray and spread evenly right to the edges of the tray. A 5mm thickness is ideal. Bake for 30 minutes or until the outer edges are crisp and brown.

Remove from oven and leave to cool for 5 mins before breaking roughly into large chunks. Serve alongside the Caramelised Beetroot Dip.

Margo + Rosa Flanagan

TWO RAW SISTERS

Rolleston, Christchurch
tworawsisters.com | @tworawsisters

You've got to nourish to flourish - wise words that Margo and Rosa Flanagan, the savvy sisters behind the brand Two Raw Sisters, now live by. They're on a mission to help Kiwis change their perception about plant-based food and teach them that good food can also be quick, affordable and delicious.

Having both struggled with personal health issues growing up, nutrition has played a key role in the Christchurch-born sisters recovery to better health. The pair were already running their own catering company before they decided to travel to Venice Beach, California and study at a plant-based culinary school to further hone their skills.

Refreshed and inspired upon their return, they began sharing their work on social media which sparked the interest of many. Now, they hit the road and travel around the country catering events, deliver cooking demonstrations, and offer workshops that cover a variety of topics such as living on a budget, under 30 minute meals, quick and easy ways to feed a family and, of course, desserts - both the raw and baked kind.

I visit the sisters at their family home in Rolleston, which serves as one of the many unique locations that they host their popular workshops from. It's a warm, relaxed setting that Margo credits is great in drawing guests out into the countryside to enjoy both a delicious and educational experience.

With bounds of energy and ambition, I'm not surprised that the young duo share with me that they are already working towards their next project - the opening of their own cooking and teaching space in inner-city Christchurch (as part of The Welder Health & Wellbeing complex on Welles Street). The Two Raw Sisters are definitely ones to keep an eye on as they continue to encourage us to go green and get creative in our own kitchens at home.

BROCCOLI BUCKWHEAT TABOULI SALAD

So simple, so easy and so delicious. We're all familiar with cauliflower rice so in this recipe we've used broccoli instead. Tender buckwheat is also the perfect grain for this salad so we encourage you to give it a try!

SERVES 8-10

⅓ cup (60g) buckwheat, *soaked overnight*

1 large broccoli, *roughly chopped*

3 stalks of kale, *leaves removed and finely chopped*

3 spring onions, *finely sliced*

Big handful of fresh herbs *(such as coriander, mint, basil)*

1 avocado, *chopped*

Handfuls of nuts/seeds of your choice *(such as sunflower, pumpkin, pistachios, almonds, sesame seeds)*

Zest and juice of 2 lemons

1 Tbsp (15ml) olive oil

Handful of goji berries

Salt and pepper, *to taste*

Green Pesto

Large handful of fresh herbs *(such as coriander, mint or basil)*

¼ cup (30g) walnuts, *roasted*

2 cloves of garlic

3 Tbsp (17g) nutritional yeast

Juice of ½ a lemon

Pinch of salt and pepper

¼ cup (60ml) olive oil

Place the chopped raw broccoli in a food processor and chop until it resembles a fine couscous like texture.

To make the green pesto, add all pesto ingredients except the olive oil into a high powered blender and pulse until a chunky mix is formed. Slowly pour in the olive oil while pulsing until well incorporated into the pesto.

Rinse and drain buckwheat then place in a large bowl with all the other salad ingredients, including the broccoli. Toss with the remaining salad ingredients until everything is well combined.

Place the salad on a large serving plate and drizzle the green pesto on top.

TIP – *This salad is delicious served with salmon!*

PEANUT BUTTER + BANANA SLICE

This 7-ingredient fudge will not disappoint. Refined sugar-free, only using ripe bananas to sweeten, this creates a slice that isn't overly sweet and leaves you with a happy tummy afterwards.

SERVES 8

Base

1 cup (120g) walnuts

1 cup (100g) desiccated coconut

½ cup (88g) dates, *soaked in boiling water for 5 minutes*

2 Tbsp (15g) cacao powder

1-2 Tbsp water

Filling

4 ripe bananas

1 ½ cups (375g) peanut butter

3 Tbsp (41g) coconut oil, *melted*

Pinch of salt

4 Tbsp (15g) cacao powder

Garnish

50g dark chocolate, *melted*

Roasted peanuts, *roughly chopped*

Place walnuts and coconut in a high powered processor and blend until a coarse flour is formed. Add the remaining base ingredients and blend until you have a dough that sticks together nicely. If it is too dry add a bit more water.

Line a 24cm x 14cm loaf tin with cling film or baking paper and press the base mixture evenly into the tin. Place the tin in the freezer to set while you make the filling.

For the filling, blend bananas, peanut butter, 2 tablespoons of coconut oil and salt in a high powered processor until you get a smooth thick mixture.

Remove the base from the freezer and pour half the peanut butter mixture into the tin. Spread out the mixture evenly with the back of a spoon. Place the slice back into the freezer to set for 2 hours.

With the other half of the peanut butter mixture add the cacao and remaining 1 tablespoon coconut oil. Blend until well combined in a high powered processor.

Once the first layer is set pour the cacao layer on top and spread evenly with the back of a spoon. Place the slice back in the freezer to set for another 2 hours.

Once the slice is set, cut into 8 bars and drizzle each slice with the melted chocolate and a sprinkle of peanuts.

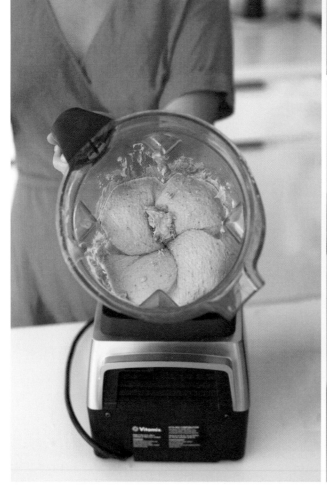

TURMERIC GREEN SORGHUM SALAD

Sorghum is a gluten-free whole grain which has a lovely chewy texture. If you can't find sorghum, brown rice or freekeh work just as well. This one bowl salad is great on its own or served with fish or chicken.

SERVES 8-10

1 cup (192g) sorghum

3 cups (750ml) water

2 heads of broccoli, *chopped into florets*

2 zucchini, *thinly sliced lengthwise*

3 Tbsp (45ml) olive oil

½ cup (75g) cashews, *roasted*

½ cup (100g) edamame beans, *shelled* or green peas

3 stalks of kale, *leaves removed and finely chopped*

1 spring onion, *finely chopped*

1 avocado, *sliced*

Big handful of fresh herbs *(such as coriander, mint or basil)*

Juice and zest of 1 lemon

1 ½ tsp ground cumin

1 tsp ground turmeric

2 garlic cloves, *crushed*

Salt and pepper, *to taste*

Place the sorghum and water into a saucepan and bring to the boil. Place a lid on top and reduce to a simmer for approximately 60 minutes. Drain and set aside to cool.

Preheat oven to 200°C and line two baking trays with baking paper.

Place the broccoli florets on one of the lined baking trays and the sliced zucchini on another. Drizzle both with olive oil and season with salt then place in the oven. Cook the vegetables for about 15 minutes on fan-bake then for the last 5 minutes change the oven function to grill. You may need to grill vegetables for a little longer depending on your oven. You want the vegetables to be nice and crispy and golden.

Once the sorghum and the vegetables are cooked and cooled, combine the two in a large bowl along with the remaining salad ingredients. Toss and season generously with salt and pepper.

Serve in the bowl or transfer to a large serving plate.

Hannah Mellsop

REAL RAD FOOD

Mt Maunganui, Bay of Plenty
realradfood.co.nz | @realradfood

Bright-eyed and beaming, I first crossed paths with Hannah Mellsop when she worked behind the counter at one of the first raw cafés in Auckland, The Raw Kitchen. Living in Auckland whilst studying Geography at university, it was during these particular years that Hannah found her curiosity drawn to the emerging plant-based scene and lifestyle. I caught a glimpse of this shift in her wellness journey as well as her colourful raw creations which she shared on Instagram and I was excited to see where her passion would take her next.

Fast forward a couple of years and Real Rad Food was formed by Hannah in 2016. She had spent an abundant amount of time working behind the scenes in various wholefood eateries and decided to take a leap of faith and serve up her own creations to the world. Specialising in creating raw, vegan treats and custom made celebration cakes that are now stocked in cafés and delivered nationwide across New Zealand, everyone is lusting for her next raw ball creation of the month or a slice of her decadent and dreamy cakes before they sell out.

Hannah decided to return home to the beautiful beachside town of Mount Maunganui to kick start her business after completing her tertiary studies. Here, she has built herself a business that continues to bloom day by day and it's a testament to Hannah's devotion and determination. I pop by her kitchen for a few hours and she's already amidst rolling some raw balls, busily wrapping up online orders to send out that afternoon and then taking more orders from her rapidly growing list of stockists over the phone.

Real Rad Food is only the beginning of great things that are still to come from the girl boss that is Hannah Mellsop.

CINNAMON DOUGHNUT RAW BALLS

Here at Real Rad Food, we specialise in creating epic and nostalgic Raw Ball flavours! This healthy take on a 'Cinnamon Doughnut' will leave your taste buds satisfied and jumping for joy.

MAKES 12 BALLS

1 cup (175g) dates, *chopped*

1 ½ cups (150g) desiccated coconut

1 ½ cups (200g) sunflower seeds

Pinch of salt

1 Tbsp cinnamon

1 tsp ground ginger

½ tsp ground nutmeg

2 Tbsp coconut sugar

2 Tbsp (30g) coconut oil, *plus extra for rolling*

Garnish

½ cup (100g) coconut sugar

½ cup (64g) cinnamon

Soak the dates in warm water for 15 minutes. Drain then set aside.

Add coconut, sunflower seeds, salt, cinnamon, ginger, nutmeg, coconut sugar and coconut oil to a food processor and blend until fine.

Continue to blend, while slowly adding in the dates as you mix. It may help to scrape down the sides a few times to ensure all the ingredients are well combined. Pour this mixture into a bowl and set aside.

Combine the garnish ingredients in another wide bowl and mix until well combined.

Add coconut oil to your hands and roll balls of the mixture into golf size balls. Then roll each ball through the garnish.

Balls will last up to 2 months in a sealed container in the freezer or a week in the fridge.

EGGPLANT +
LENTIL LASAGNE

This is a staple in our household - we've removed the pasta sheets and replaced them with eggplant to give your digestive system a well deserved break. This is the ultimate comfort food that is quick, easy, and packed with nutrients.

SERVES 4

2 Tbsp (30ml) olive oil, *plus extra for greasing and drizzling*

1 Tbsp garlic, *crushed*

1 onion, *chopped*

2 tsp smoked paprika

1 tsp cumin

2 tsp dried oregano

1 zucchini, *chopped*

1 can (400g) lentils, *drained and rinsed*

1 can (400g) diced or cherry tomatoes

2 large (800g) eggplants, *sliced into ½ cm strips*

Gluten-free breadcrumbs

Salt and pepper, *to taste*

Basil Cashew Cheese

¾ cup (112g) cashews

½ cup (114g) coconut milk

Juice of 1 lemon

200g basil leaves

2 cloves garlic

Salt and pepper, *to taste*

Preheat oven to 180°C.

Add all basil cashew cheese ingredients to a blender and blend until smooth. You may need to scrape down the sides or add extra liquid to your blender to ensure you reach the optimum consistency. Set aside.

Heat a pan over medium heat and add olive oil. Add garlic, onion, smoked paprika, cumin, dried oregano. Once onion is brown, add in the zucchini and stir.

Add lentils and the tomatoes to the pan and simmer on low-medium heat for 20 minutes. Add salt and pepper to taste.

Grease the bottom and sides of a deep baking dish with olive oil. Line the base with the strips of eggplant then pour a layer of cashew cheese, then a layer of the lentil filling. Continue layering these three components until you reach the top of your baking dish.

Top with the remaining slices of eggplant and drizzle with olive oil and sprinkle some breadcrumbs.

Bake in oven for 35-40 minutes. Allow to cool for 15 minutes before cutting and serving.

PASSIONFRUIT + VANILLA RAW SLICE

Refreshing, light and full of flavour. This raw slice is a must-have in your freezer for those afternoon sweet treat cravings. Free from gluten, dairy & refined sugars, your body will love every bite.

SERVES 16

Base

1 ½ cups (175g) desiccated coconut

1 ½ cups (200g) sunflower seeds

2 Tbsp (30g) coconut oil

Pinch of Himalayan salt

½ cup (85g) buckwheat

1 cup (175g) dates, *soaked in warm water and drained*

Vanilla Layer

2 cups (300g) cashews, *soaked in warm water and drained*

¼ cup (52g) coconut oil

½ cup (114g) coconut cream

½ cup (184g) rice malt syrup, or your choice of sweetener

1 tsp vanilla extract

Passionfruit Layer

2 cups (300g) cashews, *soaked in warm water and drained*

¼ cup (52g) coconut oil

½ cup (114g) coconut cream

½ cup (184g) rice malt syrup, or your choice of sweetener

¾ cup (170g) passionfruit pulp, *(set aside ¼ cup for topping)*

1 Tbsp turmeric

Line a baking tin with baking paper. We use a tin that is 21 x 21cm wide and 5cm high.

To make the base, add desiccated coconut, sunflower seeds and coconut oil to a food processor and blend until fine. Add in the salt and buckwheat and continue to blend, while slowly adding in the dates as you mix. It may help to scrape down the sides to ensure all ingredients are well combined.

Press this mix firmly into the base of your tin. It may help to grease your hand with some coconut oil and use the back of a spoon to smooth out the mix.

To create the vanilla layer, in the same blender add cashews, coconut oil, coconut cream, rice malt syrup and vanilla extract and blend until you reach a smooth consistency. Pour this mixture over the base layer in your tin and freeze for 15 minutes.

To create the passionfruit layer, in the same blender add, cashews, coconut oil, coconut cream, rice malt syrup, passionfruit pulp and turmeric and blend until you reach a smooth consistency. Pour this mixture over the vanilla layer.

Place in freezer to set overnight.

Carefully remove the slice from tin and use a warm knife to cut into 16 slices. Spoon the remaining passionfruit pulp on top of each slice before serving.

Store the slices in freezer for up to two months.

Shyr + Brent Godfrey

FORTY THIEVES

Stanmore Bay, Whangaparaoa
fortythieves.co.nz | @forty_thieves

The first time I tried a lick of their tasty, award-winning nut butters was at the annual Go Green Expo – one of the many events where you'll still find Shyr and Brent Godfrey proudly presenting their brand Forty Thieves in person.

After spending a handful of years residing and working in Sydney and then exploring the world, the couple returned home to New Zealand with a dream to venture into the food industry. They were equipped with little experience but a strong desire to develop an artisanal and nutritious product that complemented their passion for health and fitness. Their luxurious nut butters now feature in stores nationwide, boasting bright and bold eco-friendly packaging (designed by Shyr herself) and thoughtfully sourced, heart-healthy ingredients.

Their unique line-up of spreads features mouthwatering flavours such as Salted Macadamia, Hazelnut Crunch and Scorched Almond. It is inspiring to learn that they also offer the supply of pails of their fresh nut butters to like-minded businesses such as wholefood cafés and caterers. Ensuring accessibility to all those who value incorporating delicious, nutritious, and wholesome ingredients in their everyday lives is an aspect Shyr highlights that they work hard towards fostering as a business.

Based on the Hibiscus Coast for both home and work, the pair particularly enjoy the supportive community in this region as well as the natural beauty of the coast on their doorstep. We take a break to enjoy the view and sit down to tuck into the hummus spread with warm pita bread in hand – a meal heavily inspired by Shyr's Israeli background. With the name Forty Thieves itself inspired by an adventure packed tale (of Ali Baba and the Forty Thieves) – Shyr and Brent's journey so far, I think, is also a fitting reflection of just that.

CRISPY CAULIFLOWER SALAD

WITH SATAY DIPPING SAUCE

Creating crispy cauliflower can be a challenge without a deep-fryer.
Try our unique blend of almond milk and rice flour to create a
delicious coating that comes out crispy when baked.

SERVES 2

Crispy Cauliflower

2 Tbsp oil

2 Tbsp rice flour

4 Tbsp almond milk

½ tsp salt

1 small head of cauliflower,
   chopped into florets

Satay Dipping Sauce

3 Tbsp Forty Thieves Crunchy
   Peanut Butter

1 ½ tsp soy sauce

2 tsp coconut sugar

4 Tbsp coconut cream

½ red chilli, *finely chopped*
   (or ¼ tsp chilli flakes)

½ tsp ginger, *grated*

Green Salad

1 cup baby spinach

1 radish, *thinly sliced*

½ cup fresh mint, *chopped*

½ cup coriander, *chopped*

1 Tbsp sesame oil

1 Tbsp apple cider vinegar

½ tsp salt

1 tsp sesame seeds

Preheat oven to 180°C and line a baking tray with baking
paper.

Combine the oil, rice flour, almond milk and salt in a medium
sized bowl to create a wet paste. Mix thoroughly until there
are no lumps. Add in the cauliflower florets and completely
coat the pieces in the batter. Cover the bowl and leave in the
fridge for 10 minutes.

To make the satay dipping sauce, mix the peanut butter and
soy sauce in a bowl. Add in the coconut sugar and coconut
cream until well combined. Then mix in the chilli and ginger.

Remove the cauliflower florets from the fridge and lay them
evenly onto the baking tray without letting the pieces touch
each other (this will ensure the cauliflower comes out crispy
and not soggy when baked).

Place in the oven for 10 minutes or until golden and then
turn the pieces to cook on the other side for an additional 10
minutes. Once cooked, remove from the oven and allow to
cool for 2-3 minutes.

To make the salad, toss together spinach, radish, mint and
coriander. Whisk together the sesame oil, apple cider vinegar
and salt before mixing this through the salad.

Divide the salad between two large plates and sprinkle
the sesame seeds on top. Top each salad with the crispy
cauliflower florets.

Drizzle the satay sauce over the salad or serve in a ramekin on
the side for dipping the cauliflower in.

TRADITIONAL HUMMUS – THREE WAYS

Crafting the perfect hummus comes down to 3 things: freshness of the chickpeas, quality of the tahini and the toppings to tie it all together. Keep the base simple and experiment with different toppings.

Hummus Base

150g dried chickpeas, *soaked overnight, drained and rinsed*

½ tsp baking soda

4 cups (1L) boiling water

4 Tbsp Forty Thieves Hulled Tahini

1 ½ Tbsp lemon juice

2 cloves garlic, *chopped*

¼ tsp salt

½ tsp cumin

3 Tbsp ice water

Place chickpeas into a large pot and place on a low heat. Stir continuously with a wooden spoon for 2-3 minutes. Add baking soda and continue mixing for another 2-3 minutes. You should see the chickpeas start to soften.

Add in boiling water to the pot and let cook for 30-40 minutes or until soft. Scoop out any skins or scum that rises to the surface.

Once cooked, drain chickpeas (a cooked chickpea should squash easily between your thumb and forefinger).

Add cooked chickpeas to high powered blender. (If you are making the traditional topping, set aside ½ cup of chickpeas before you do this, to be used as garnish.) Blend on high speed for about 5 minutes until a paste is formed.

Add tahini, lemon juice, garlic, salt and cumin. Blend for another 3 minutes, slowly adding the ice water until desired texture is reached.

Divide the hummus between three bowls.

Traditional Topping

½ cup (80g) cooked chickpeas, *set aside from hummus base*

1 egg, *boiled and peeled*

1 Tbsp pine nuts

Fresh parsley, *chopped*

Olive oil, *to serve*

½ tsp sweet paprika

Traditional Topping

Scoop the leftover ½ cup chickpeas onto the centre of a plate filled with a base of hummus.

Cut the boiled egg in half long ways. Place the egg on top of the hummus yolk side up.

Sprinkle with pine nuts and parsley. Generously pour a swirl of olive oil over the hummus and dust with paprika.

Beetroot + Mint Topping

1 cup (150g) beetroot, *washed, peeled, and chopped into 3cm pieces*

1 Tbsp olive oil

¼ tsp salt

¼ tsp white pepper

Fresh mint, *chopped*

1 Tbsp sesame seeds

Olive oil, *to serve*

Beetroot + Mint Topping

Preheat oven to 180°C and line a baking tray with baking paper.

In a bowl, toss beetroot, olive oil, salt and pepper and mix with your hands until beetroot is coated evenly.

Place onto the tray and bake for 30 minutes or until cooked. Be sure to turn beetroot over half way through the cooking time.

Gently pile the beetroot onto the centre of a plate filled with a base of hummus. Garnish with mint and sesame seeds and generously pour a swirl of olive oil over the hummus.

Garlic Mushroom Topping

2 Tbsp olive oil

1 clove garlic, *crushed*

5 button mushrooms, *quartered*

½ tsp cumin

¼ tsp salt

Fresh parsley, *chopped*

Olive oil, *to serve*

Garlic Mushroom Topping

Heat oil in a pan and fry the garlic. Add in mushrooms then cumin and salt and cook for another 5 minutes or until mushrooms are soft.

Pile the mushrooms onto the centre of a plate filled with a base of hummus. Garnish with parsley and generously pour a swirl of olive oil over the hummus.

ALMOND BUTTER, PEAR + GINGER LOAF

This loaf is super simple to throw together before inviting friends over for afternoon drinks. Deliciously moist, each bite offers chunks of fragrant pear, sharp ginger and moreish chocolate.

MAKES 1 LOAF

2 eggs

½ cup (100g) coconut sugar

½ cup (125ml) rice bran oil

3 Tbsp Forty Thieves Smooth
    Almond Butter

½ cup (120g) sour cream

½ cup (60g) wholemeal flour

¾ cup (75g) rolled oats

1 tsp baking soda

¼ tsp salt

2 ripe pears

½ cup (90g) dark chocolate,
    coarsely chopped

½ cup (115g) crystallised ginger,
    chopped

Preheat oven to 180°C. Grease the bottom and sides of a regular sized loaf tin and line with baking paper.

In a small bowl, beat together eggs and sugar for 2-3 minutes or until the mixture becomes thick and fluffy. Stir in oil, almond butter and sour cream.

In a large mixing bowl, combine flour, oats, baking soda and salt. Create a well in the dry ingredients and pour wet ingredients into the centre. Mix until well combined.

From the base of one pear, slice 4 even rounds ½ cm in thickness and place aside. This will be used to decorate the top of the loaf. Be sure to remove seeds. Chop the remainder of the pear as well as the second pear into 3cm chunks.

Add pear chunks, chocolate and ginger pieces into the cake mixture and mix until combined. The mixture will be quite thick.

Pour mixture into the loaf tin and smooth out the surface. Lay the sliced rounds of pear on the top in a line.

Bake for 40-50 minutes or until skewer inserted comes out clean.

Remove from the oven and let cool for a few minutes before turning out onto a wire rack.

James Denton

GOODFOR

Auckland
goodfor.co.nz | @goodforstore

James Denton is an entrepreneur at heart. Previously, he took on a food truck in Queenstown with a few of his mates, serving up freshly pressed, soft-shell tacos. He'd discovered the art of making a great tortilla in Mexico - one of the many stops along his adventure travelling and working around the world upon finishing university. But it wasn't long before his ambition led him to dream up his next business venture - New Zealand's first zero-packaging, bulk foods store, GoodFor wholefoods refillery.

GoodFor was started by James in a bid to lead a more sustainable life and encourage others to do the same by reducing the use of plastic packaging when it comes to purchasing our pantry staples. His approach was to make it a trendy, easy and convenient experience for us and it has been a promising one.

In March 2017, Ponsonby, Auckland saw the opening of the first GoodFor store. I still clearly remember the day I stumbled upon the store with a friend. Clean, crisp and simple - it's a slick space fit for foodies and environmentalists and I found myself wandering round in circles in awe of all that was on offer. Stocked with a vast range of organic, mostly locally-sourced ingredients, it's also a really inspiring place to visit when you're looking for alternatives or you feel like getting a little experimental with your meals.

With four stores across New Zealand, and plenty more in the works, GoodFor is a great new way for us to shop that, as the name suggests, is good for the people and the earth. From nuts, seeds and grains to cooking oils and syrups, you can also fill up on household cleaning products that are on tap alongside your dose of kombucha and peanut butter. Gather together your empty jars and reusable bags, head into GoodFor and help be the change in the world (in style!).

FISH TACOS
(TACOS DE PESCADO)

Born from a surf trip in Puerto Escondido, Oaxaca, Mexico, these tortillas filled with exotic flavours will be a lifelong favourite. Lightly pan-fried fish with sweet, pink pickled onion, and a zesty tartare all upon a freshly pressed tortilla.

SERVES 4

Tartare Sauce

½ cup mayonnaise

Juice and zest of 1 lemon

1 pickled gherkin, *diced*

2 Tbsp gherkin juice

2 Tbsp capers, *diced*

Filling

1 red onion, *thinly sliced*

Juice of 1 lemon

Fish

3 juniper berries

1 Tbsp smoked paprika

1 tsp cayenne pepper

1 tsp salt

½ tsp pepper

Zest of 2 lemons

400g firm white fish *(such as Tarakihi)*

Olive oil, *for cooking*

Tortillas

2 cups (300g) masa flour
  (50% maseca, 50% minsa)

1 cup (250ml) water

Pinch of salt

To serve

½ a purple cabbage, *thinly sliced*

Bunch of coriander, *roughly chopped*

To make the tartare sauce, in a bowl stir together all the sauce ingredients and salt and pepper to taste. Cover and refrigerate.

To prepare the filling, combine red onion and lemon juice in a bowl. Massage with your hand for 1 minute and leave to sit on the bench as you prepare the remaining ingredients. Turn/stir over occasionally.

To prepare the fish, grind all spices and the lemon zest together in a mortar and pestle. Slice the fish into pieces roughly 12-14cm in length and 2cm in width. Rub the fish thoroughly with the spice mixture. Cover and refrigerate for 20 minutes.

To make the tortillas, combine masa flour, water and salt together in a bowl. Mix well then lightly knead for 1 minute. Roll the dough into 30g balls (golf ball size).

Press each dough ball using a tortilla press or roll out with a rolling pin to 1.5mm in thickness. Place one at a time into a medium heated pan, turn after 20 seconds to seal each side and continue to turn after 20 seconds for 3 turns. The best result is for them to puff with steam in the middle after the second turn. Stack cooked tortillas on a plate and cover with a tea towel to keep them warm and moist.

Heat a pan with oil to a medium heat, add the fish and pan-fry the fish for 45 seconds on each side or until just cooked.

To serve the tacos, place a bed of cabbage, top with pickled onion, a piece of warm fish and a dollop of tartare sauce and a garnish with coriander.

SPAGHETTI VONGOLE

After living on the southern French and Italian border, I quickly became obsessed with the Italian classic, Spaghetti Vongole. Its sweet, simple flavour combined with the incredible texture of the fresh pasta is a real treat every time.

SERVES 4

2 ¾ cups (400g) 00 Bakers flour

4 eggs

2 Tbsp salt

¾ cup (190ml) extra virgin olive oil

4 cloves garlic, *diced*

1 bunch Italian flat leaf parsley,
  roughly chopped

3 cups (480g) fresh clams,
  *scrubbed clean on the outside
  and any barnacles removed*

½ cup (125ml) white wine *(such
  as Pinot Gris)*

1 can (400g) cherry tomatoes

½ tsp dried chilli flakes

½ cup (45g) parmesan cheese,
  grated

Place flour in a mixing bowl. Make a well in the centre, crack the eggs into it and beat lightly with a fork.

Using your hands, mix the eggs with the flour, a little at a time, until everything is combined. Knead the dough together and keep kneading/pulling/stretching until it feels soft and silky.

Wrap the dough in cling film completely and refrigerate for 30 minutes.

Starting with the widest setting, roll the pasta through a pasta roller, adding dustings of flour to the exterior as you go. Continue to lower the settings and roll until it is almost transparent and then finally roll it through the "spaghetti setting".

Bring a large pot of water to the boil and add 2 tablespoons salt.

Meanwhile, heat a pan to a medium heat with 2 tablespoons of olive oil. Add garlic and half of the parsley, then very quickly add the clams and the wine. Toss everything together a few times and then add in cherry tomatoes, chilli flakes and the remaining olive oil. Cook until the clams just open. Let this sit while you quickly cook the pasta.

Add the fresh spaghetti to the pot of boiling water and cook for 2 minutes or until al dente.

Drain the pasta then pour into the pan with the vongole sauce and mix everything together until the pasta is well coated.

Garnish with parmesan and remaining parsley then serve.

TIP – *If you don't have a pasta machine, not to worry! You can hand roll your pasta with a rolling pin and cut into strips with a knife or pizza cutter. This process just takes longer and requires a little more strength. Once your spaghetti is ready, dust with flour to prevent the noodles from sticking to each other.*

STICKY FUDGE BROWNIE

Everybody loves a brownie and a lot of people are pretty particular about how they like theirs. I like mine really rich and extra gooey and this is exactly how this brownie should be!

MAKES 10-12 SLICES

1 ½ cups (260g) dark chocolate buttons

¾ cup (190ml) coconut oil

Sea salt, *to taste*

1 cup (200g) coconut sugar

3 eggs

3 Tbsp oat flour

2 Tbsp cacao powder

½ tsp baking soda

½ tsp baking powder

4 medjool dates, *chopped*

½ cup walnuts

To serve

1 cup (175g) dark chocolate buttons, *melted*

Walnuts, *roughly chopped*

Coconut yoghurt, ice cream or whipped cream

Preheat oven to 180°C and line a baking dish with baking paper.

Create a bain-marie by placing a glass or steel bowl over a pot with boiling water in it (don't let the bottom of the bowl touch). Add in the chocolate buttons, coconut oil and a pinch of salt. Allow ingredients to melt and stir frequently.

In a separate bowl, beat together coconut sugar and eggs. Add oat flour, cacao powder, baking soda, baking powder, medjool dates and walnuts and fold together - be careful not to over-mix.

Add the chocolate from bain-marie into this mixture and fold through until just combined.

Pour the mixture into the baking dish and bake in the oven for 12-20 minutes (depending on how high the mixture sits in the baking dish).

Remove from the oven and allow to rest for 10 minutes.

Gently melt the dark chocolate buttons over a bain-marie. Drizzle this on top of the brownie and sprinkle over a handful of walnuts.

Serve warm alongside coconut yoghurt, ice cream or a dollop of whipped cream.

Zara + Shinee McIntyre

HALF BAKED CATERING

Tawa, Wellington
halfbakedcateringco.com | @halfbakedcateringco

The McIntyre sisters love to occasionally indulge in a delicious treat like most of us do. So much so that they want to prove that you can satisfy your sweet cravings and feel good about it too. Thus, Half Baked Catering was founded by Zara and Shinee McIntyre and raw, vegan, refined sugar-free treats as well as beautiful baked cakes (hence the name Half Baked) are their specialty.

The bustling capital that is Wellington is brimming with good food, freshly roasted coffee and its fair share of cafés. It is also the city that the two sisters call home. Before Half Baked Catering came to be, both Zara and Shinee grew up working alongside their father at the iconic Cuba Street café, Midnight Espresso. Naturally, they grew familiar with the ins and outs of hospitality over the years but, behind the scenes, they also discovered a love and talent for crafting sweet treats.

Come 2016, the duo decided to take their cue, branch out on their own and share their creations with the world - inspiring the launch of Half Baked Catering. They took inspiration from their own journey and experience in discovering healthier options when it comes to food and intertwined this with their appreciation for desserts. All of their mouth-watering creations are plant-based, handcrafted and use natural ingredients that are organic and locally sourced where possible - it's a win-win for both us and Mother Nature.

The sisters are constantly experimenting with new flavours and ideas and supply to a handful of stockists as well as the locals throughout the Wellington region. Keep an eye out for their delectable range of frozen dessert bars in-store too, aptly named 'Snicky Fingers' and 'Maui Wowee' - a wholesome take on the classic and much-loved Snickers and Bounty Bar that will delight you with each and every bite. Which will be your pick?

HEMP, CACAO +
MACA SMOOTHIE

One of our favourite smoothies to make, and drink!
This nutty, chocolatey treat is perfect for any time
of the day, even breakfast!

SERVES 1

1 banana, *frozen*

2 ice cubes

3 Brazil nuts

2 tsp almond butter or nut
  butter of your choice

3 heaped tsp cacao powder

2 tsp maca powder

1 tsp hemp protein

½ cup (125ml) filtered water

½ cup (125ml) coconut milk or
  milk of your choice

¼ cup (60ml) hemp milk

Garnish
Cacao nibs
Hemp hearts

Combine all ingredients except cacao nibs and hemp hearts
in a blender on high speed, blend until smooth for about a
minute.

Pour into a large glass and add a sprinkle of cacao nibs and
hemp hearts. Serve chilled.

AVOCADO LIME CHEESECAKE

This 'cheesecake' is the perfect summer dessert. The nutty
base and zesty lime complement the creamy avocado perfectly.
It will keep in the fridge for up to 2 weeks, if it lasts that long!

SERVES 12
MAKES ONE 18CM CAKE

Base

¼ cup (35g) roasted almonds

¼ cup (21g) desiccated coconut

¼ cup (33g) sunflower seeds

¼ cup (25g) ground almonds

¼ cup (70g) date paste

½ Tbsp coconut sugar

Seeds from ½ vanilla bean

2 tsp coconut oil, *melted*

Pinch of salt

Filling

2 cups (290g) cashews, *soaked
overnight*

1 cup (250ml) filtered water

1 cup (240g) coconut butter,
softened

Juice and zest of 3 limes

1 Tbsp (15ml) lemon juice

½ cup (125ml) rice malt syrup or
maple syrup

Seeds from ½ vanilla bean

Pinch of salt

1 cup (250ml) coconut oil

½ tsp matcha powder *(optional)*

1 ripe avocado

Candied Lime Slices

1 lime, *sliced thinly*

1 tsp coconut sugar

To make candied lime slices, coat the slices with coconut
sugar. Cut out a piece of baking paper to fit in your
dehydrator and lay slices out flat. Dehydrate on medium
setting overnight.

To make the base, in a food processor combine the first four
ingredients until a fine consistency is achieved. Add date paste,
coconut sugar, vanilla, coconut oil and salt and combine well.
Spray an 18cm springform or removable bottom cake tin and
evenly press the base mix into the tin. Place in the freezer for 10
minutes.

While the base is chilling, add cashews and water to a food
processor and blend for 5 minutes until smooth, scraping down
sides with a rubber spatula. Add the remaining filling ingredients
except for the matcha powder (if using) and avocado. Blend for
a further 2 minutes. Remove 1 cup of mixture and refrigerate;
we will use this later for the topping.

Add avocado and matcha to remaining mixture and blend for
another 2 minutes (you may need to add more water until
it reaches a pourable consistency). Remove the base from
the freezer and pour this mixture on top. Place back in the
freezer and leave overnight.

The next day, remove the leftover cup of mixture from the
fridge and leave it to sit for about 20-30 minutes or until
it starts to soften. Place it back in the food processor and
blend till smooth and creamy. Transfer to a piping bag fitted
with a large nozzle.

Remove cake from freezer and leave to sit for 5 minutes
before removing from cake tin. Pipe the cream topping as
desired and decorate with candied lime slices.

Leave to defrost for a further 15 minutes before cutting
with a hot knife. Serve chilled and keep any remaining cake
refrigerated.

BANANA, WALNUT + CARAMEL CAKE

The combination of flavours in this delicious cake is definitely one of our favourites! We've included extra caramel in this recipe so there's enough to also drizzle on each serving.

SERVES 12
MAKES THREE 18CM CAKES

1 cup (250ml) coconut cream

1 cup (250ml) liquid coconut oil
  or light olive oil

½ cup (125ml) coconut milk

½ cup (125ml) filtered water

Seeds from ½ a vanilla bean

2 large ripe bananas, *mashed*

1 tsp salt

3 cups (405g) gluten-free flour

1 ½ cups (225g) coconut sugar

1 tsp baking soda

2 tsp baking powder

1 tsp cinnamon

½ cup (55g) walnuts, *chopped*

Coconut Cream Whip

2 ½ cups (625ml) full fat coconut
  cream *(refrigerated overnight)*

Seeds from ½ a vanilla bean

1 Tbsp coconut sugar

¼ tsp guar gum

¼ cup (60ml) coconut oil, *melted*

Caramel Sauce

½ cup (125ml) coconut cream

¼ cup (60ml) coconut milk

¾ cup (112g) coconut sugar

1 Tbsp coconut oil

Pinch of salt

Candied Walnuts

1 Tbsp coconut sugar

1 tsp water

½ cup (55g) walnuts, *chopped*

Pinch of salt

Preheat oven to 170°C. Spray and line three 18cm cake tins.

Combine coconut cream, oil, coconut milk, water, vanilla and bananas in a cake mixer or with a hand beater on medium speed. Sift salt, flour, sugar, baking soda, baking powder and cinnamon into a bowl. Combine the two mixtures, along with the chopped walnuts. Divide and pour the mixture between the three lined cake tins.

Bake for 30 minutes. Leave to cool before removing from tins and transferring to a wire cooling rack.

To make the candied walnuts, in a small saucepan on low heat, dissolve the coconut sugar in the water until melted, stirring continuously for about one minute, let bubble for 10 seconds and remove from heat immediately. Add walnuts and mix until thoroughly coated and the sugar starts to set.

Spread out flat on a lined baking tray and sprinkle with salt. Leave to cool for a minute or so then crumble with hands.

To make the coconut cream whip, separate the coconut milk from the coconut cream. In a mixer or with a hand beater starting on medium speed, whip the coconut cream, vanilla, coconut sugar and guar gum for 5 minutes or until it starts to thicken.

Reduce speed to medium and slowly pour in coconut oil (making sure it is at room temperature) and mix until combined.

To make caramel sauce, combine ingredients in a small saucepan. Bring to the boil, stirring continuously. Reduce heat and simmer for 10 minutes stirring every 2 minutes. Leave to cool.

To assemble the cakes, make sure they are fully cooled (at least 2 hours). Trim the top of the cakes if needed. Beginning with a layer of cake, top with ⅓ of the coconut cream, drizzle ⅓ of the caramel sauce and sprinkle ⅓ of the candied walnuts. Repeat with remaining layers.

Ben Warren

BEPURE

Havelock North, Hawke's Bay
bepure.co.nz | @bepurebenwarren

Ben Warren is a man on a mission. Originally from Bath, England, he has spent the last 15 years working as a clinical nutritionist. He now shares his wealth of knowledge, most notably by touring and presenting seminars right around New Zealand. He is also the founder of BePure - a holistic, nutrition company with a clinic based in Auckland. Here, Ben leads a team of holistic health consultants to help support the health of New Zealanders.

I jumped at the opportunity to attend one of Ben's talks a few years back, intrigued to listen to his thoughts on the topic of 'discovering how to be healthy and happy in the modern world'. Incredibly passionate and well spoken, Ben ignited a conversation about how to listen, understand and fuel our body according to our own needs. To best understand what we each need to fuel and thrive on, we need to delve into our genetics - a unique concept that is the heart of the BePure philosophy.

Alongside his ever expanding team at BePure, Ben is devoted to helping us uncover and understand the crucial role food and nutrition play in our lives. Educating and empowering the community to adopt simple, mindful practices and find optimal health is a stark difference to the time spent earlier on in his career teaching professional golf but I doubt that Ben would change a thing.

Ben and his wife Lynda take me for a stroll in the fierce sun through his 15-acre farm in Havelock North. We go in search of juicy, homegrown berries - the perfect garnish on top of the Gut Loving Marshmallow Lynda's whipped up. His schedule keeps him on his feet but when Ben isn't travelling around the country or abroad, he returns here to his organic, permaculture farm to spend time with Lynda and their two young daughters - roaming around foraging for ingredients to inspire their next family meal.

SEASONAL GO-TO RICE SALAD

This is one of those throw-it-together-at-the-last-minute salads. The key to getting lots of greens in this salad without anyone objecting is to chop the kale or chard really finely!

SERVES 4

1 cup (195g) brown basmati rice

2 cups (500ml) boiling water

1 Tbsp butter or coconut oil

1 zucchini, *thinly sliced*

1 carrot, *grated*

½ red capsicum, *chopped*

½ red onion, *chopped*

5 kale or Swiss chard leaves, *stripped off the stem and finely chopped*

Large handful of roasted peanuts, or any nut or seed of your choice

Optional extras

Parsley, *finely chopped*, dried cranberries or raisins, peas, blanched sugar snap peas, beetroot, *grated*

Dressing

½ tsp ground ginger

1 tsp curry powder

1 garlic clove, *crushed*

1 tsp honey

3 Tbsp olive oil

3 Tbsp apple cider vinegar or lemon juice

Salt and pepper, *to taste*

Place rice and boiling water in a medium saucepan and cook covered for 20 minutes or until rice is done. Place aside to cool.

While the rice is cooking, melt butter in a large frying pan and cook the zucchini in a single layer. When the slices start to brown on one side, flip them over and brown the other side. Set aside to cool.

In a large serving bowl, combine the cooked rice, zucchini and the remaining salad ingredients including the optional extras, except the peanuts.

To make the dressing, place all dressing ingredients into a small jar and shake vigorously to combine, pour over the rice salad and stir well.

Sprinkle the peanuts over the salad just before serving.

GOOD-FOR-YOU GREEN SAUCE

With at least 12 different green herbs in it, this is great for making sure you are feeding your biome with a variety of herbs. Use more or less of each herb as you have them available. Don't forget things like dandelion and puha will make it quite bitter.

MAKES ABOUT 500ML

1 cup (60g) *firmly pressed* parsley and/or coriander

¼ cup (15g) nasturtium leaves

¼ cup (25g) rocket

12 leaves (25g) dandelion

7 leaves (15g) puha

10 leaves (10g) plantain

5 leaves (15g) mizuna

Handful (20g) of lamb's-quarters

10 leaves (60g) Swiss chard or silverbeet, *stripped off the stalk*

2 leaves (15g) kale, *stripped off stalk*

Small handful (10g) of sage

5 stems (40g) rosemary, *stripped off the stalk*

3 ½ Tbsp (30g) capers

2 cloves of garlic

6 heads of calendula flowers

½ cup (125ml) olive oil

½ cup (125ml) apple cider vinegar

1 tsp salt

Place all the ingredients into a high powered blender and blend until smooth.

Pour into a jar for storage and drizzle extra olive oil over the top for extra preservation.

This sauce is great drizzled over meats, as a spread on toast, or on crackers with cheese, avocado and egg. You could also stir through rice or pasta or even use it as a dip with crudités.

GUT-LOVING MARSHMALLOW

This marshmallow is fabulous because it contains gelatin which is great for gut healing. It is tasty with a fantastic fluffy texture - kids will love it.

MAKES 10-12 SLICES

3 Tbsp gelatin

½ cup (125ml) cold water

½ cup (125ml) boiling water

1-2 Tbsp honey, *to taste*

1 tsp vanilla extract

1 tsp freeze-dried berry powder,
   optional

In a small bowl, mix gelatin and cold water together then set aside to bloom for 2 minutes.

In a large bowl dissolve the honey in the boiling water then add the bloomed gelatin and stir to dissolve.

Whisk with an electric mixer for 5-10 minutes until the mixture is white and foamy and you achieve a ribbon like texture.

Add vanilla and beat for another 30 seconds. Then stir in the freeze-dried berry powder if using.

Pour the mixture into a baking dish and smooth out the surface right away - be sure to move quickly as it sets fast!

Rajeev Joshi + Graedon Parker

ORGANIC MECHANIC

La Cigale Markets, 69 St Georges Bay Road, Parnell, Auckland
organicmechanic.co.nz | @theorganicmc

If you have ever stopped by the La Cigale Markets in Parnell, chances are you will have heard of the Organic Mechanic. Greeted by infectious good vibes and some of the best hugs in the world, Graedon Parker along with friends Rajeev Joshi, Alex Leu and brothers Nick and the late Jason Corliss, have taken residence here since 2013 serving health-affirming elixirs from their 'OM Shack'. I'll never forget the day our paths crossed and my friendship with them has been the catalyst that inspired my own deep fascination with finding health and wellness.

At a time when smoothies weren't really associated with health, Organic Mechanic were serving them up to the community fresh, every weekend at the markets. The idea for their stall began on the back of a conversation between school friends Graedon and Jason who were both influenced by Mike Corliss' (Jason and Nick's father) diagnosis with cancer and his journey to seek how to help heal his body naturally before his passing.

Continuing on the path towards better health, Organic Mechanic decided to try their hand at brewing kombucha. The bubbly, fermented beverage rich in probiotics is now one of their signature products - locally made in small batches, organically produced by hand and stocked and served in stores and cafés nationwide. But it's not all about the drinks - the guys have never been shy about dreaming big and their initiatives have seen them give back to their community by launching schemes such as #smoothiesinschools (offering low decile schools the opportunity to be introduced to and taught about the health benefits of consuming fresh smoothies).

With an entire tribe of friends and followers behind them, there is no denying the strength and power of Organic Mechanic as true ambassadors for holistic health and a conscious approach to business in the changing landscape of our food industry.

BAKED CURRY POTATO CAKES
WITH VEGAN BUTTER SAUCE

These curry cakes are well worth the effort and the sauce is every bit as good as the regular. The cakes can be enjoyed on their own, served in a burger, or chopped up and thrown into a salad.

SERVES 4

Baked Curry Potato Cakes

4 potatoes, *peeled (optional) and chopped into medium-sized cubes*

1 carrot, *peeled (optional) and chopped into medium-sized cubes*

2 Tbsp cooking oil

1 tsp mustard seeds

1 tsp cumin seeds

2 tsp curry powder

½ an onion, *finely diced*

½ tsp salt

Vegan Butter sauce

½ an onion, *finely diced*

2 Tbsp cooking oil

2cm piece of ginger, *finely diced*

3 cloves garlic, *finely diced*

1 dried chilli

½ tsp salt

1 Tbsp paprika

1 Tbsp curry powder

1 Tbsp ground cumin

½ tsp garam masala

2 ½ Tbsp coconut sugar

1 can (400g) of chopped tomatoes

1 ½ tsp dried fenugreek leaves

¾ can (300ml) of coconut milk

Preheat oven to 200°C and line a baking tray with baking paper.

Boil the chopped potatoes and carrots in water until they are soft enough to mash. Turn off the heat and drain the water.

Heat the oil in a pan over medium heat. Add mustard seeds and cumin. When the mustard seeds start to pop, add curry powder, onion, salt, potatoes and carrots.

Mix all the ingredients in the pan ensuring the carrots and potatoes are covered in the spices. Turn heat on high and fry the potatoes and carrots for 1-2 minutes to get them crispy.

Turn off heat and mash the mixture in the pan.

Form the mixture into patties and place on the lined baking tray. Place in the oven to cook for 5 minutes on each side or until the surface is golden and crispy.

To make the butter sauce, fry onions in oil on low-medium heat for 5 minutes. Add ginger, garlic and chilli and fry for another 2 minutes.

Turn the heat down to low and add salt, paprika, curry powder, cumin, garam masala and sugar and cook for 3-5 minutes. Keep stirring the mixture to make sure it doesn't burn.

Add in tomatoes and fenugreek and place a lid on the pan and cook for 20 minutes. Then add in the coconut milk and simmer for another 15 minutes.

Serve the baked potato cakes hot with a scoop of butter sauce on top. You can also serve alongside some cucumber yoghurt raita *(see page 160)*.

CUCUMBER YOGHURT RAITA

A cooling condiment to balance out the heat of typical Indian dishes. Try serving this alongside the baked potato curry cakes.

MAKES 1 CUP

¼ cucumber, *sliced thinly lengthwise*

1 ½ tsp salt

3 pinches of cumin seeds

Pinch of turmeric powder

Pinch of paprika

4 mint or coriander leaves, *finely chopped*

1 cup (250ml) coconut yoghurt

Place sliced cucumber in a bowl and add salt, cumin seeds, turmeric, paprika and mint and toss.

Let sit for 10 minutes then stir in coconut yoghurt.

Garnish with a pinch of paprika and turmeric.

MASALA CHAI TEA

Being born and raised in New Zealand, food was one of the few ways I was able to connect with my Indian heritage. This is a dairy-free version of the classic tea enjoyed by many every day. Brewed with ginger and warming spices, this one will help to get the inner fire burning.

SERVES 5-6

Large piece of ginger (15-20cm), *grated*

6 cups (1.5L) water

5 Tbsp sugar

3 tsp loose-leaf black tea or 4 teabags

4 tsp chai spice

1 cup (250ml) coconut milk

Combine ginger, water, sugar, tea and chai spice in a pot.

Bring to the boil and let boil for 10-15 minutes.

Strain the tea into another pot.

Add coconut milk, stir and gently bring to a boil. Turn off heat just before bringing the mixture to boil.

Pour into cups and serve hot.

TIP – *You can use the leftover ginger and tea to make another 1-2 boils of this tea.*

Hannah Jack

COUNTRY KITCHEN

Kaukapakapa, Auckland
countrykitchen.co.nz | @countrykitchennz

Out amongst the bed of marshmallow root and echinacea flowers is where you will likely find Hannah Jack. Tending to her field year round, these are the herbs and flowers that lend their medicinal powers to Hannah's popular organic skincare products – all which are handcrafted here on her small rural farm in Kaukapakapa.

Having grown up in the area, Hannah chose to also raise her young family here whilst running her own business, Country Kitchen. Look around and you'll spot a breathtaking view of rolling hills, a thriving vegetable patch out back that keeps the family well fed, and the walls in her home studio are lined with jars upon jars of botanical infusions. It's a tranquil setting perfect for Hannah to work from and host workshops all while being able to watch over her two young sons who are never too far away exploring the great outdoors.

From body oils to lip tints, face creams to perfumes, all her products are thoughtfully produced in small batches with some herbal oils slowly infused for months. The plants themselves are nurtured with organic and sustainable methods which takes plenty of care and patience, and the same can be said of Hannah's approach to food. A few years prior, before Country Kitchen launched as a skincare range, Hannah's passion for sustainability and wholefoods had inspired her to create raw cakes and treats to share with the locals at the weekend markets.

As we sip on chamomile tea freshly brewed with the flowers from last season's harvest, Hannah goes about delicately pressing petals into each of the shortbread cookies before we pop them into the oven and wait for the perfect accompaniment to our herbal tea. It is clear that there is nowhere else Hannah would rather be than with a basket full of flowers by her side.

STRAWBERRY + MACADAMIA RAW TARTS

These tarts have a perfectly balanced taste and texture with the biscuit-like base and the creamy strawberry filling. You can use any other berries that are in season or more sustainably harvested in the area that you live.

MAKES 16 TARTS

Macadamia Base

2 cups (256g) ground almonds

1 cup (150g) macadamia nuts

Zest of 2 lemons

1 Tbsp coconut oil, *melted*

5 medjool dates

Strawberry Filling

1 ½ cups (225g) raw cashews,
  soaked for 1-3 hours

1 cup (250ml) coconut cream

1 vanilla pod, *scraped* or
  2 tsp vanilla extract

¼ cup (60ml) lemon juice or the juice
  of 2 lemons

¼ cup (60ml) coconut oil

1 cup (150g) strawberries

¼ cup (60ml) maple syrup

To serve

Coconut yoghurt

Fresh, dried or freeze-dried flowers

Line a muffin tray with baking paper or grease the tray with coconut oil. Alternatively, silicone muffin trays work well for this recipe.

To make the tart base, blend macadamia nuts and almonds in a high powered blender. Add the lemon zest, coconut oil and medjool dates. Pulse until well combined.

Line the individual tart trays with the mixture, making sure the mixture comes up the sides of the muffin trays as much as you can. Place the tray in the freezer to set.

To make the creamy filling, process cashews and coconut cream in the blender and blend until smooth. It will take about 5 minutes to get this silky. To test this, rub a little of the mixture between your fingertips; it should feel like velvet and glide between your fingers. If it feels gritty, keep blending. Add in the remainder of the filling ingredients and blend until smooth.

Remove the bases from the freezer and fill the cases up with the filling. Place tarts back in the freezer until set, about 2-3 hours.

To serve, remove tarts from the freezer and allow to defrost for 15 minutes. Decorate each of the tarts with a dollop of coconut yoghurt and either fresh, dried or freeze-dried strawberries or wild strawberry leaves and flowers.

TIP – *Lay a thin strip of baking paper at the bottom of each muffin cup to make removal of the cakes easier.*

ALMOND + ROSE SHORTBREAD
WITH PRESSED FLOWERS

Presenting a tin of beautiful biscuits to guests over tea is incredibly heart-warming and humbling, especially biscuits with delicate pressed flowers and a soft hint of rose.

MAKES ABOUT 30 COOKIES

200g butter, *unsalted and softened*

⅔ cup(135g) unrefined icing sugar

1 tsp rosewater

½ vanilla pod, *scraped* or 1 tsp vanilla extract

1 ½ cups (192g) plain flour

1 cup (128g) ground almonds

Pinch of salt

Flower petals or herbs, (*violas and pansies work well)*

Glaze
1 egg white

2 Tbsp rosewater

Unrefined caster sugar, *for dusting*

Preheat oven to 150°C and line a baking tray with baking paper.

Beat together butter and sugar. Pour in rosewater and vanilla and beat again until incorporated. Sift in flour, then add ground almonds and salt. Beat again until you get a soft pliable dough.

Roll out the dough to 1cm thick in between two baking sheets. Place in the refrigerator for 30 minutes to harden.

Take the dough out of the fridge, take off the top baking sheet and cut the dough into desired shapes and sizes with a knife or cookie cutter. Press your flowers into the dough and then place the baking sheet back over the dough and roll over it again with a rolling pin to make sure your flowers are pressed in well. Place back into refrigerator for another 30 minutes.

Remove from the refrigerator and place the cookies onto the lined baking tray.

To make the glaze, in a small bowl whisk together the extra rosewater and egg white. Brush over the biscuits and dust with a little sugar.

Bake for 7-10 minutes or until the sides only just start to turn golden brown.

Store any remaining cookies in an airtight container.

CALENDULA, ORANGE + CARDAMOM CAKE

When oranges brighten up winter with their radiant hues amongst the evergreen landscapes I cannot help but make this citrus cake that is infused with warming cardamom. I adore juicing the calendula flowers in with my oranges to encompass their medicinal qualities and bright energy that is appreciated at this time of the year but this step can be left out if this is not possible to do so.

SERVES 8-10
MAKES ONE 23CM CAKE

Juice of 3 oranges

3-4 fresh calendula flowers

½ cup (120g) butter, *unsalted and softened*

½ cup (64g) rapadura sugar

2 eggs

1 cup (250ml) coconut milk

1 tsp apple cider vinegar

¼ tsp ground cardamom

1 cup (128g) stoneground, spelt or gluten-free flour

1 cup (128g) ground almonds

½ tsp baking soda

1 tsp baking powder

Raw Chocolate Drizzle

50g cacao butter

1 Tbsp coconut oil

4 Tbsp cacao powder

1 Tbsp maple syrup

Pinch of salt

Garnish

Calendula flowers, *optional*

Prepare your bundt tin by buttering the sides then dusting a gentle amount of flour around the sides. Tip out any left over flour. Buttering around the edges of the tin is important and gives your cake a beautiful buttery crust.

Preheat the oven to 180°C.

Juice oranges and your calendula flowers. In a bowl, beat together the butter and sugar. Add your eggs one at a time and continue to beat well.

Fold in coconut milk, orange and calendula juice and cider vinegar. Sift, then fold through cardamom, flour, ground almonds, baking soda and baking powder and pour into your tin.

Bake for 20-25 minutes or until a skewer comes out clean when inserted through the middle of the cake.

Over a bain-marie, combine cacao butter, coconut oil, cacao powder, maple syrup and salt. Slowly melt together then take off the heat. Continue to stir until the cacao mixture thickens. You can refrigerate this for a few hours to let it harden a little.

Once the cake is cooled, remove the chocolate drizzle from the fridge and drizzle over the cake. Finish by scattering over calendula flowers.

Alesha Bilbrough-Collins

BEARLION FOODS

Shop 3, 78 Brighton Mall, New Brighton, Christchurch
bearlionfoods.co.nz | @bearlionfoods

A simple, rustic space paired with organic, locally sourced and seasonally inspired fare is what you will discover at BearLion Foods. After venturing around the world working in kitchens in London and Melbourne, Alesha Bilbrough-Collins (the lion) and her husband John (the bear) returned home inspired to launch their own delicatessen in New Brighton, Christchurch.

Having originally trained as a chef in Christchurch, each week, Alesha designs a menu that offers sweet and savoury options and takes care to cater to those with food allergies. Big on flavour and respect for sustainability, there is something for anyone and everyone who stops by.

Big, glorious platters of salads are freshly prepared in the early hours of each day and are waiting behind the glass cabinets. The sweet treats are a-plenty too - I take my pick and opt for a delightfully moist cashew and date cake generously drizzled in star anise and espresso syrup. Bold, unexpected flavour combinations seem to be Alesha's signature take on the food offered here at BearLion Foods – it's both an intriguing and refreshing sight. A peek inside the fridges also reveals an assortment of handmade preserves, pickles, spreads, and plant-based milks – most of which are on offer at the Christchurch Farmer's Market come Saturdays.

BearLion Foods first found its feet as a stall at this weekly farmer's market located in the beautiful, historic grounds of Riccarton Bush. Since branching out to their current seaside shop-front, it's provided Alesha with the opportunity to also host cooking classes after hours and special late-night dinners and offer catering – all in a commitment to educate and excite people's palates with good, honest, wholesome food.

MISO ROASTED POTATOES

WITH PEA TAHINI AND HERBS

Miso is such a handy ingredient I always make sure it's in the fridge. Try the potatoes on their own as a side or the pea tahini also makes a great dip or accompaniment to fish or lamb.

SERVES 6-8

6 medium potatoes, *chopped with skins left on*

½ cup (150g) miso paste

½ cup (125ml) water

3 Tbsp olive oil

Pea Tahini Dressing

4 cups (500)g peas *(set aside 2 cups for tossing whole with potatoes)*

½ cup (150g) hulled tahini

½ cup (125ml) water

¼ cup (60ml) lemon juice

2 tsp salt

To serve

6 cloves garlic, *sliced thinly*

¼ cup (60ml) olive oil

1 tsp chilli flakes

1 cup (100g) fresh herbs *(such as coriander, basil or mustard leaf)*

2 Tbsp poppy seeds

Preheat oven to 200°C and line a baking tray with baking paper.

Mix miso, water and oil to make a paste. Toss potatoes in this paste making sure they are all evenly coated.

Place on the lined baking tray and roast in the oven for 20-30 minutes or until tender. This step can be done ahead of time if you wish.

While the potatoes are roasting, make the pea tahini by placing all the ingredients in a bowl and use a hand blender to mix until smooth, or any blender alternatively.

In a small saucepan, combine garlic and oil and cook on a medium heat until it starts to turn golden brown. Pour this over the potatoes and add in the 2 cups of remaining peas and chilli flakes. Lightly toss so the garlic oil has dressed everything and season with salt.

In a large serving bowl, layer the potatoes first, drizzle some pea tahini, herbs then poppy seeds. This salad is best served at room temperature for maximum flavour.

ROASTED BEETROOT + KŪMARA

WITH RHUBARB AND HORSERADISH YOGHURT

I have always adored rhubarb and I love finding ways of using it without boiling it with heaps of sugar. Using it in salads is a great option as it adds a sour note that pairs stunningly with sweet kūmara.

SERVES 6-8

6 medium sized beetroots

4 Tbsp apple cider vinegar

2 large kūmara, *roughly chopped*

Salt and pepper, *to taste*

4 Tbsp olive oil

4-6 stalks of rhubarb, *roughly chopped*

Horseradish Yoghurt Dressing

1 cup (245g) natural unsweetened yoghurt

2 Tbsp horseradish paste

1 tsp salt

Garnish

½ cup (100g) walnuts, *lightly roasted at 170°C in the oven for 15 minutes then roughly chopped*

Preheat oven to 200°C.

Place beetroots in a small roasting dish and ⅓ fill with water, cover with foil and poke a few holes through the foil before roasting in the oven for about 40-60 minutes. To check if the beetroots are cooked, use a sharp knife to pierce them. If it goes through easily then it's cooked, if you feel resistance cook for a little longer.

Once cooled, cut the tops off and any other hard bits. No need to peel; just cut into rough shapes and splash with the vinegar and a pinch of salt.

Rub the chopped kūmara with oil, salt and pepper. Place on a lined baking tray and roast with beetroot until golden brown and tender.

Once oven is free, turn it up to 220°C, scatter rhubarb evenly on a tray and place in oven for only 5-8 minutes. You want it to still hold its shape but be soft and tender.

To make the yoghurt dressing, mix horseradish and salt with yoghurt. If you are lucky enough to find fresh horseradish then just grate it straight in.

In a large serving bowl, place beetroots on bottom first then the kūmara, using up any of the residual oil that may still be on the roasting tray. Drizzle the yoghurt evenly over then scatter rhubarb and roasted walnuts.

TIP – *Try pairing this salad with roast duck or pork.*

BAKED YOGHURT CHEESECAKES

WITH PLUM AND BLACK CARDAMOM

I've always been a fan of cheesecakes but as my diet slowly changed to all things real, cream cheese started to freak me out as it is such a heavy ingredient. Using yoghurt makes it so much lighter and actually a fantastic alternative breakfast treat.

MAKES 6 INDIVIDUAL CAKES

Base

5 cups (150g) cornflakes

5 cups (100g) puffed rice

⅓ cup (80ml) coconut oil, *melted*

½ tsp cinnamon

¼ cup (50g) hemp seed or hemp flour

Filling

3 eggs, *room temperature*

⅔ cup (75g) coconut palm sugar, *grated*

2 cups (450g) plain yoghurt, *room temperature*

Topping

1 kg stoned plums

1 ½ cups (250g) coconut sugar

1 Tbsp ground black cardamom

Cashew Butter Topping (optional)

2 cups (300g) cashews, *roasted*

⅓ cup (80ml) coconut oil, *melted*

Generous pinch of salt

Place all base ingredients in a food processor and process until fine and well combined. Pack this mixture into 6 individual moulds or greased muffin trays. Place in the fridge to set for 30 minutes or until firm.

Preheat oven to 150°C.

To make the filling, whisk together all the filling ingredients in a bowl until sugar is dissolved. Use your fingers to help dissolve any sugar lumps that remain in the mixture.

Pour filling evenly between moulds. Place in the oven for 15-20 minutes. Remove from the oven and check with a calm shake of the tray. You still want a little movement in the middle of each cake, as residual heat will keep cooking them.

Once the cakes have cooled place in the fridge and let set overnight. Remove from moulds the next day.

To make the topping, place all the topping ingredients in a pot and bring to a boil, turn down on low and let simmer and reduce by half. Let cool.

To make your own cashew butter, simply blend all ingredients in a high powered blender till creamy and smooth. Spoon over some cashew butter onto each cake before topping with stewed fruit if using.

TIP – *You can also make this recipe as one large cake. Cooking time may take another 10 minutes or so.*

Damian Chaparro

ARO HĀ WELLNESS RETREAT

Glenorchy, Queenstown
aro-ha.com | @damianchaparro

Nestled outside the quiet town of Glenorchy in the Southern Alps, you will find the luxurious wellness retreat that is Aro Hā. Once inside the sparse yet warm timber interior of the main lodge, the magnificent view of Lake Wakatipu welcomes you. I find myself taking in a moment of solitude and stand in awe of the sheer beauty of our New Zealand landscape. Aro Hā is built upon the philosophy of slowing down and encouraging more mindfulness into our lives. But don't be fooled – days spent here are filled with plenty of yoga, hikes amongst the subalpine surroundings, and permaculture and cooking classes.

Aro Hā is the brainchild of Damian Chaparro and his business partner Chris Madison – both whom have spent plenty of time at retreats themselves and first crossed paths at one in California. Years were spent dreaming, planning and researching as well as scouting for the perfect location before eventually, the pair built their vision of a retreat here on a site that is only a 40 minute drive from the vibrant heart of Queenstown.

As the morning fog slowly lifts, Damian and I wander through the on-site gardens which provide fresh, organically grown ingredients for the plant-based, paleo-inspired menu served to guests on the week-long retreats. Together, we harvest some baby bok choy and romanesco for his deconstructed sushi bowl. Damian has taught yoga for the past 16 years and now concentrates on guiding the retreats here at Aro Hā - he confides that the resident chefs would be genuinely surprised to find him here in the kitchen cooking on a day like this.

Before I head home, I've also fallen in love with the idea of Biophilia - a concept favoured by Damian (who has co-created a wellness festival of the same name) which refers to the healing power of Mother Nature. While the mesmerising surroundings reconnect you with the present moment, the rainbow of creative, delicious plant-based fare that awaits you at Aro Hā will also transform your body and mind.

DECONSTRUCTED SUSHI BOWL

If I had to choose a country to eat from for the rest of my life, it would be Japan. Known for plant-based diets, an intimate relationship with the sea, and one of the oldest living populations in the world, this dish embodies the flavours and benefits I love.

SERVES 4

Pickled Cucumber

1 cucumber, *thinly sliced*

½ cup (125ml) rice wine vinegar or apple cider vinegar

2 tsp coconut sugar

1 Tbsp tamari

1 tsp sesame oil

2 Tbsp sesame seeds

Red Rice

2 cups (400g) red or brown rice

¼ cup (60ml) sushi rice vinegar

Teriyaki Roasted Cauliflower

6 Tbsp tamari

¼ cup (60ml) water

3 Tbsp rice wine vinegar

2 tsp ginger, *grated*

4 Tbsp coconut sugar

1 Tbsp cornstarch

1 head cauliflower, *chopped into florets*

8 small carrots

Salt and pepper, to taste

Olive oil

4 baby or 2 medium sized bok choys, *thinly sliced lengthwise*

To serve

½ pack of nori sheets, *cut diagonally into triangles*

4 radishes, *thinly sliced*

Coriander, *to garnish*

To make the pickled cucumber, place sliced cucumber in a bowl and sprinkle with a generous pinch of salt – gently mix. Set aside for 5 minutes then rinse and drain.

In a lidded container, combine rice vinegar, coconut sugar, tamari, sesame oil and sesame seeds. Add cucumbers to the container and with the lid on, toss to marinate.

To make the rice, cook rice as per package instructions. Once cooked, add sushi rice vinegar and stir well to combine.

To make the teriyaki roasted cauliflower, preheat oven to 200°C.

Add tamari, water, rice wine vinegar, grated ginger and coconut sugar into a medium pot. Bring to boil and simmer on low heat for 5 minutes. Dissolve cornstarch in a small amount of water. Add this cornstarch mixture into the pot to thicken, mixing well. Simmer for a further minute and stir occasionally. Add cauliflower to the pot and toss to combine.

Spread cauliflower in a single layer on a lined baking tray.

Place carrots on separate lined baking tray. Sprinkle generously with salt, pepper and olive oil. Roast both the cauliflower and carrots in the oven for 20 minutes or until done.

To sauté the bok choy, heat olive oil in a pan over medium heat. Add bok choy and season with salt and pepper. Cook for a few minutes.

To serve, add a scoop of rice, some toasted cauliflower, bok choy, carrots, pickled cucumber, a couple of nori sheets and some radish in a serving bowl. Garnish with coriander and extra sesame seeds.

SHAKSHUKA

This is healthy comfort food. Cook once, eat twice, as it keeps beautifully. I'll even take it to potlucks so we can all sit around saying "shakshuka"!

SERVES 4

1 shallot, *finely sliced*

Olive oil

3 red or yellow capsicums,
  thinly sliced into strips

3 cloves garlic, *thinly sliced*

2 tsp smoked paprika

1 tsp ground cumin

¼ tsp cayenne pepper

3 400g cans of chopped tomatoes

Salt and pepper, *to taste*

6 eggs

1 handful parsley, *chopped*

100g goat's feta

To serve

Pita pockets, *toasted*

Preheat oven to 200°C.

In an oven-safe frying pan, sauté the shallots in the olive oil on medium heat for about 2 minutes.

Add in capsicum and cook for a further 5 minutes. Add garlic, paprika, cumin, cayenne pepper and cook for a further 2 minutes. Add in the cans of tomato and stir to combine. Season with salt and pepper to taste and bring to a simmer for a further 15 minutes, or until slightly thickened.

Using a large spoon, create small wells in the sauce and crack an egg into each well. Repeat until all eggs are used. Sprinkle parsley and crumble feta over the top.

Place the pan in the oven and bake until the egg whites are just set, about 12-15 minutes. The eggs will continue to cook slightly as the dish cools.

Serve the shakshuka with toasted pita pockets that are perfect for dipping into and a simple side salad if you wish.

NEW MEXICAN EGG POCKETS

Where I'm from, Santa Fe, New Mexico, eating is an excuse for getting more chilli into your life. This is one of my go-to breakfast recipes. Gluten-free, low carb and delicious, this meal keeps blood sugar low and energy levels stable.

SERVES 4
MAKES 12 POCKETS

1 head iceberg or cos lettuce

12 eggs, *poached*

Large handful of coriander

Micro greens, *optional*

Guacamole

2 avocados, *mashed*

180g cherry tomatoes, *diced*

½ an onion, *diced*

1 Tbsp chilli powder

Juice of 1 lime

Salt and pepper, *to taste*

Meaty Mushroom Filling

4 large Portobello mushrooms or
   600g of any mushrooms, *sliced*

¼ cup olive oil

2 cloves garlic, *minced*

1 tsp smoked paprika

Juice of 1 lime

Pinch of salt

2 tsp chilli powder, *or to taste*

Green Chilli Pesto

1 cup pumpkin seeds, *toasted*

2 Tbsp nutritional yeast

2 cloves garlic, *peeled*

Juice of 1 lime

1 Tbsp apple cider vinegar

2 tsp chilli powder, *or to taste*

1 handful fresh basil

1 handful parsley

Drizzle of olive oil

Salt and pepper, *to taste*

To make the meaty mushroom filling, heat a pan over high heat. Combine the sliced mushrooms, olive oil, minced garlic, smoked paprika, lime juice, salt and chilli powder. Cook for about 5 minutes.

To make the guacamole, in a small mixing bowl, toss together all the guacamole ingredients and set aside.

To make the green chilli pesto, place the all the pesto ingredients into a food processor or blender and blend until mixed yet chunky.

To serve the egg pockets, in each lettuce cup, layer mushrooms, guacamole, a poached egg and a spoonful of pesto. Garnish with coriander and micro greens if using.

TIP – *You can also use corn or whole wheat flour tortillas to serve instead of lettuce cups.*

With thanks

Thank you to everyone in this book for being a part of this story and inspiring this particular chapter. It has been an unforgettable experience travelling around the country I will always call home - to collaborate with you, exchange stories while we cook, get creative and bring to life ideas like this to share with our family, friends and community.

Sally Greer and Rachel White, thank you for being there when I was ready to take the leap again, for your constant support and trust in my vision. It has been a pleasure to work with you both to pen another beautiful book.

Dad and Mum, thank you for always being there - especially to pick me up in the middle of the night and drop me off in the early hours of the morning while I travelled back and forth and across the ditch for this project.

To my friends who have been so wonderfully encouraging, letting me bounce my ideas and thoughts off you and helping me out in all the small ways - thank you.

Lastly, thank you if you are here reading this, if you are here because you loved my first book WHOLE. And to my family, friends and to all those who have shared, recommended or treated someone special to a copy of my book – you've got good taste!

xo

Index